Many Roads to Love

True Stories of How Couples Meet and Make Their Love Last

Betty Lucas

Many Roads™

Printed in the United States of America.

For information about Many Roads to Love or special discounts for bulk purchases, visit www.manyroads.net.

Lucas, Betty.

Many Roads to Love, True Stories of How Couples Meet and Make Their Love Last

ISBN: 0-9774029-0-8

Credits

Artwork: Dan Schlesinger
Design: Marilyn Cadiz
Editor: Trevor Rogers
Publisher: Many Roads

Dedication

I dedicate this book to Bruce Springsteen, whose lyrics portray life's frailties and reveal what it takes to make love last. I am grateful to him for his many words of wisdom that guided my husband before we met, and that continue to serve as inspiration for us both.

Thank you, Bruce Springsteen.

Acknowledgments and Thanks

Many Roads to Love is a tribute to those who so willingly shared their lessons and lasting devotion. I extend my heartfelt appreciation to all who contributed their stories.

I want to thank many additional folks. My son, Trevor Rogers, provided invaluable editing expertise. Katherine Salazar-Poss kindly helped with her legal advice. Dan Schlesinger donated his marvelous cover art. Tripp Mikich worked wonders with his photo editing.

My niece, Jocelyn Smeltzer, added ongoing enthusiasm for the project. I received wonderful support and encouragement from my family (all nine brothers and sisters), as well as friends and colleagues: Cinda Rosenburg, JoAnn Scordino, Bev Mire, Patty Brink, Connie Anderson, Caro Pemberton, Sharon Miller, Hallie Warshaw, Ann Mead, Allison Neves, Annamarie Harris, Todd Lyckberg, Richard Zorab, and Gail Nyman York.

I am grateful to every previous love for the many lessons I learned along the road that led me to my husband, Stephen Golub. He has provided ongoing inspiration and guidance for this book and continues to offer his unwavering support for each of my endeavors.

Thank you all.

About the Contents of Many Roads to Love

Every road to love is unique. So rather than artificially categorizing and dividing the following stories into separate sections, I intersperse stories about different kinds of couples and experiences throughout the book. Whether the reader chooses to skip among stories or read the book from start to finish, a variety of themes and subjects will emerge: first-time love, traditional love, alternative lifestyles, and lessons from seasoned couples. All stories, however, share one common theme: lifelong commitment.

At the back of the book, you will find a "Toolbox of Tips" that I have compiled, for singles seeking love and for couples who are challenged in their relationships.

Betty Lucas

Introduction

I compiled this book to inspire singles seeking love and couples looking to make love last.

The book springs from my own search for inspiration. Throughout my life, I longed to discover the secrets of lasting love. As a young adult my role models for relationships came from the movies, not from real life. I wanted to believe in "happily ever after." But I secretly wondered how two people—regardless of how much love they shared—could awake together each day and not tire of each other eventually. I hungered for healthy examples.

So while still single in my early forties, I began collecting real-life love stories for what became this book. I gathered them through casual conversations, interviews, and small notices I placed in newspapers. Even though I doubted that my own life would become such a story, each true tale of a successful relationship inspired me. I decided to produce a book filled with such tales and inspiration.

Several years and hundreds of how-we-met stories later, I remain moved by each tale of success and by learning what makes love last. Not surprisingly, some common themes span the stories selected for this book, illuminating attributes and practices of happy long-term couples. Their lessons range from fresh perspectives to tried-and-true advice. Regardless of longevity or circumstance, each couple displays a steadfast, life-long commitment.

Contrary to popular belief, love alone rarely suffices to sustain a couple. Over time, every relationship demands time and attention. Working on it must become as natural as eating and drinking—both partners must keep nourishing their love to keep it flourishing.

I met my wonderful husband in 1998, a few years after starting this project. Had I not maintained my interest in relationships and diligently collected these stories, I doubt I would have taken the steps that eventually led to our meeting and marriage. Our story closes this collection.

There are countless books that offer advice on achieving healthy, loving relationships. No matter how many I read, I find that the most valuable lessons stem from true stories of success rather than focusing on how to fix what's broken. I hope that this book inspires people to wait for or recognize the right partner, work to make a relationship thrive, and, above all, see that there are many roads to love.

"At first I read every book I could find, looking for warranty information, any signs that the joke would be on me—to finally love someone only to have him come complete with a life-threatening condition."

Love in a Perilous Climate

Catherine and Alex, Alaska

It's quite possible that I just didn't get a good look at him the first time. Mid-December in Alaska is a shadowy, twilit time of blues and purples that can make even a robust person seem to dissolve into the surroundings.

To this young college student from the temperate East Coast, the weather had an added effect—it turned me inward. I wasn't necessarily saddened by the sub-arctic twenty-hour nighttime, but I began to imagine myself taking on the slow, antlered qualities of moose. I found myself ruminating in notebooks and losing track of where I was in my classes. I wasn't dating. I had little interest. For fun I was doing things like tossing a bowl of hot water into minus forty-degree Fahrenheit air and watching it sublimate—turn to twinkling crystals, then air, without ever returning to the ground.

My friend Carla, also from out of state, was dealing with the chill by constantly eating chocolate-chip cookie dough and seducing quiet boys. One evening, Carla needed more butter. As a gesture of goodwill, she called three friends who needed to go to the store as well. Alex was her latest male "friend," and he was already in the backseat when she picked me up. I slid in beside his modest silhouette, feeling the down stuffing of our parkas brushing together, sleeve against sleeve. There was an introduction, I think. I asked him some questions to try and spark a conversation, but our words were much like that bowl of hot water, evaporating in the space above us. It was the wrong season. It wasn't the right time.

Carla kept me informed of her adventures with Alex. One day she told me things had ended with him, and then paused. "You know?" she said, "You should date Alex! He's a really nice guy."

"No, no thanks," I responded.

Was it just too much trouble? Was I lazy? What would I do with a "really nice guy" while my mind was on all the exciting and unstable young men that slipped past me in the university hallways? Not everyone is as slow to mature as I was—some nineteen-year-old girls really do know what they want—but I wasn't one of them.

Skip forward almost seven years. I'd finished college, driven around the continent with only my dog as a companion, made countless fits and starts at romance, and finally decided that Alaska was the closest approximation to home territory I could find. I took a veterinary job two miles from the first college I had attended, and I lived in an ancient, drafty cabin in an adjacent town called North Pole. (Sending Christmas cards from there is always fun.)

A coworker told me her fiancée's brother was lonely. Not those exact words, of course. For three months I kept his phone number on a scrap of paper on my refrigerator. It was the first thing I saw every morning, and nearly the last thing at night. Still, I did nothing.

When I finally called, we talked like nervous strangers, bartering information tit for tat. I am an only child. He is one of eleven. Turned out the whole batch of them grew up in North Pole. Turned out we both liked ice cream. Turned out he wanted to be an actor and I wanted to be a writer.

It was late June when we finally re-met. As mythically frigid and dim as interior Alaska can become in the winter, it erases even the cruelest memories of cold with its summers. The valleys sprawl wide and green against the horizon. Twenty hours of daylight are capped off with a crimson-gold color that skims the hills at 2 a.m., from a sun that never truly sets. Upon pulling into the drive where we met for our first late-night ice cream, this was the light he was swathed in—a kind of glow, an omen of arrival.

Our first date lasted a few hours. Two days later we went hiking, and that date lasted twenty-four hours. We drove four hundred miles in the summer light, to Denali National Park and back. I was talking about something unimportant when Alex blurted out, "And speaking of sex, when was the last time you had any?"

"We weren't talking about sex," I corrected.

"Huh." He mulled this over. "Well, we are now." Then that mischievous smile emerged.

I can't decide where to weave it in, the detail that Alex and I began dating only ten months after he had undergone a liver transplant for a congenital disease. (He was very pleased to find that the important parts of his 'plumbing' stilled worked—quite smoothly!) At first I read every book I could find, looking for warranty information, any signs that the joke would be on me—to finally love someone only to have him come complete with a life-threatening condition.

There was one episode during which Alex spiked a fever, and another where it became high enough to warrant a trip to the hospital. I put ice packs under his armpits and drove him to Fairbanks as I cursed into the open air outside the driver's side window. But he hung on and got stronger. And I stopped looking for more information on the human liver and started concentrating on the human business of living.

The transplant is not part of our day-to-day story now, except for yearly checkups and some tiny pills. He has an enormous scar that carves up both sides of his abdomen and peaks under his sternum, where the disease was removed and replaced by something healthy. Perhaps that is analogous to what happened in those seven years between when I first met Alex and when we reconnected—I suffered some scars, but managed to replace something unhealthy with something healthy and was ready for love.

How We Make Our Relationship Last

What makes a marriage work? Good grief, don't ask me! I only know about my partnership, and how we got to where we are. It has something to do with recognizing the frailty and temporality of life, looking honestly at my own behavior before pointing fingers, speaking up about expectations, and listening before resentments can build. Discussing spirituality together also helps. It's about timing, and celebrating a good thing once you've found it because, of course, any of us could have our lives cut too soon. I expect that with some prayer and work, things only get better and better as life progresses.

Love in a Perilous Climate

"I couldn't make up my mind whether she was interested in me or just looking for a place to live."

Not Enough Hot Water
Chris and Nirit, Israel

*I*t was that miserable period between fall and winter when London really is not at its best. I had spent the entire previous summer traveling around the United States, and was now trying to settle in for my second year of college. London seemed especially drab after California and New York.

One of my flat-mates and I were on our way to the movies. I can't remember what film was showing, but we were certainly going far out of our way to see it: Golders Green, a suburb in the north of the city. We were waiting for the 73 bus on Tottenham Court Road when I noticed a strikingly attractive girl at the bus stop. Mark, my flat-mate, had seen her too. He nodded in her direction.

"Italian," I said, assuming that her dark features and long hair were Neapolitan. No sooner had I spoken than she looked straight at us, took a few steps toward me, and asked, "Does the 73 bus go to Muswell Hill?"

I wasn't sure, but feigned local knowledge and told her that it did. Just then, the bus arrived; we all boarded and went upstairs. This was back when smoking was still allowed on the upper decks of London buses. Mark and I sat on one bench seat, with the "Italiana" behind us. She and I began talking, and I learned that she was actually an Israeli from Haifa.

The next thing she said was, "I'm looking for a place to live. Do you have any spare rooms at your house?" Quite a startling thing to ask an English gentleman.

She explained that she was boarding in someone's house in Muswell Hill, but wanted to move out. Well, living arrangements at our place were complicated, what with two guys and three girls sharing, but I asked her to give me her phone number in case I heard of anything.

So I now had her name—Nirit—and a phone number. I thought about her often, and wondered if I should phone.

A few weeks later, another friend of mine told me he was looking for a flat-mate. He was living in an up-market apartment building in Bloomsbury but couldn't afford the rent. I dug up Nirit's phone number and we arranged to meet that evening. The rendezvous was near the 73 bus stop, where we had first met. She wasn't impressed with my friend or his apartment, but we went out for some dire English cuisine nearby. She paid. I couldn't make up my mind whether she was interested in me or just looking for a place to live.

Another month went by, maybe longer, and my flat-mates were planning a party. We had inherited this particular house from a gang of final-year students and it had a reputation for outrageous parties—a reputation we were trying to maintain. Impulsively, I decided to phone Nirit and invite her.

Parties are terrible places to try to get to know someone. However, I recall some attempt at intimacy before I lost consciousness. This obviously failed to dim her liking for me, because we arranged to meet the following Wednesday at a pub on Goodge Street. The atmosphere at the pub was more conducive to socializing. At the end of the evening, she popped the question in a very forthright manner: "Your place or mine?"

It had to be her place, since there was no room for privacy at mine. Off we went to Muswell Hill. I remember being shocked by the amount of clothes she owned. What on earth could one person do with so much apparel? In the morning I suggested sharing a bath—my idea of romance at the time—but this being England, there wasn't enough hot water to fill the tub.

Between the two of us, however, it turns out that there was and continues to be enough love to raise three children and fill 25-plus years of marriage.

Not Enough Hot Water

How We Make Our Relationship Last *(Nirit's version)*

The secret of our relationship is the respect and space we give each other. Neither of us tries to change the other. As for me, every time I get upset with some little thing that comes between us, I always remind myself why I married Chris. Not because he thinks, behaves, or acts like me, but because he thinks, dreams, and lives differently. I don't force him to like my friends (although he does—which I love), and I don't expect from him things that are not in his nature to give.

I take what he gives and love being his best friend. He enjoys his space and loves to travel and have his own experiences, which is why I fell in love with him all those years ago. We don't have to be the same. We respect each other's differences. I need my own time with my friends, work, and social life. Chris never tries to change me. When all is said and done we find it more fun to do the things we like together, as friends, rather than as husband and wife.

How We Make Our Relationship Last *(Chris's version)*

It sounds very old fashioned, but from my point of view the main reason we have a successful relationship is because we married, and we married so we could raise a family.

Yes, we were in love, and it was a love driven by passion and excitement and everything else that seems important when you're in your twenties. But I think there's something in the DNA that kicks in when you start making babies, or when you cradle your firstborn in your arms.

We still love one another, but I accept that it's love of a different quality than the love we felt 25 years ago. Having a family and being blessed with three wonderful kids has been a much bigger adventure than a relationship limited to the two of us could ever have become.

Just before the wedding, we each received marital advice from our respective parents. Nirit's Mom told her, "When your man comes home, first of all make sure he eats." My Father's wisdom was, "Whatever your wife wants, first agree to it, then try to negotiate." Sounds corny, but it seems to work.

We have both been very generous to one another and we try not to be selfish. We've watched plenty of other relationships fall apart and it makes us appreciate how lucky we are.

Not Enough Hot Water

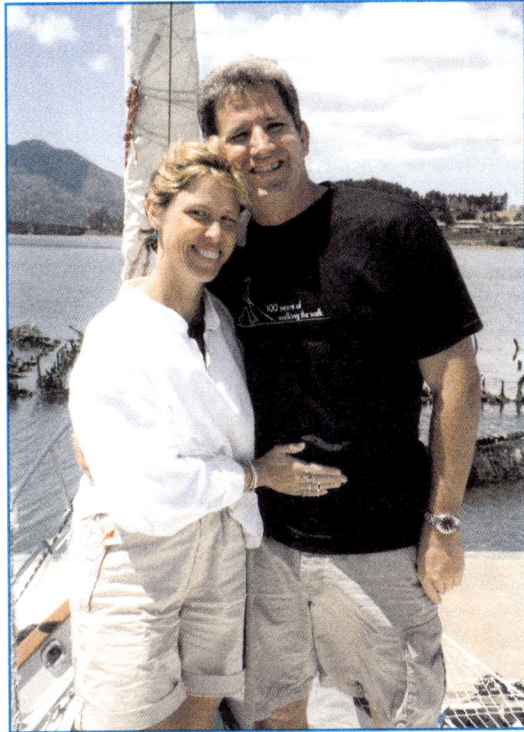

"We don't focus on how to make it last but rather how to make it right for both of us."

Throw Caution to the Wind

Pam and Scott, on the water somewhere

"If you need a place to stay, you can stay at my house," I told my coworker Scott. It really was nothing more than an innocent gesture from a colleague—Scott and I were working for collaborating agencies. He was married, commuting from a neighboring city. I had recently divorced and was offering my coworker a place to stay.

Over a period of fourteen years, our paths crossed both socially and professionally. Scott came and went as a result of his ever-changing career position.

Eventually, Scott and his wife separated. For the first time, Scott and I were working together and were single. We are also both legally blind (meaning we have very limited sight). Since our offices were side by side, we began to discuss our personal lives more and more. I was heavily into the online-dating scene. Every week I would share stories with Scott about how I met various guys. Scott's limited experience with online ads was not positive. He had placed an ad, hoping to meet people to sail with, and ran into some real creeps.

Every so often, Scott would ask me to go sailing. Finally, we went sailing together with two coworkers and a friend. We had a great time. I remember my coworker remarking the next day, "You know, Scott's personality would be good for you because he is silly and easygoing." I immediately thought: no way, we're just friends.

The next day I stopped in the office with my latest date in tow. This was when, according to Scott, "the psychological torture of Scott" began. Scott invited me to go sailing, but I suggested my date might like to go instead. Scott ended up sailing in the morning with my date.

One Monday I returned to the office after an evening yoga class and found Scott still working. He and I decided to go out for dinner. We talked more about online dating. I advised Scott to give it a try. Scott says that he thought I was subtly hinting that I desired something more than friendship between the two of us. That was when, he says, the lines between friendship and a romantic relationship began to blur in his mind. I remained clueless concerning his shifting feelings, and pursued my dating escapades.

Since it was late and Scott would have had to take the bus all the way to Sausalito (where he was living), I once again offered my house. Scott declined. As he puts it, "Here I was being offered a perfect opportunity to confess my feelings, but I chickened out."

The next morning I awoke to find an e-mail addressed to "Sailing-gal" (my online-dating pen name). The subject line was "Throw lots of caution to the wind." I was intrigued because it was a great twist on my personal ad titled: "Throw caution to the wind."

"If I'm barking up the wrong tree, I can take it," the e-mail said. Further down, the sender had written, "If our coworkers have been picking up vibes, it's probably because of me."

That's when I realized who had written the e-mail. Scott had created a profile online, found my ad, and was confessing his feelings for me online. I immediately turned off the computer in shock. As I proceeded to get ready for work, it occurred to me that I needed to reply or I would not be able to face him. So I turned the computer back on and briefly replied, "I would be willing to chat about this." We got together that evening and admitted a mounting mutual attraction for each other but I wasn't ready to pursue it.

Throw Caution to the Wind

By this time in my dating adventures, I happened to have become smitten with a new guy I'll call "John." To make matters worse, I had already invited John to join Scott and me on a sailing trip. Considering my growing feelings for Scott, I was totally confused. I really liked John, but now I knew Scott was interested. We agreed to stick with our original sailing plans, thinking, naively, that it would all somehow sort itself out.

Well, our sailing date was a disaster. Scott tried not to look me in the eye. He stared straight ahead sailing the boat while John was all over me, demonstrative as he could be. When the day was done, I was exhausted and more confused than ever.

I knew I needed a break to sort out my feelings. I couldn't deny that I was beginning to think of Scott as a romantic interest after more than fourteen years of friendship. The last thing I wanted to do was destroy our friendship, but how would I know if there was something between us if I didn't take the risk? I decided to take a risk, say goodbye to John, and act on my growing affection for Scott.

It proved to be a difficult transition. We had to sort out all the many layers of complications that arise when two executives in the same company move from being friends to being lovers.

Scott's dream was to be the first legally blind person to sail around the world. Before I met Scott, my dream was to crew a boat and, of course, sail off into the sunset with the man I loved. Together, both our dreams came true. In September 2004, we sailed under the Golden Gate Bridge as the first legally blind couple to embark on a sailing adventure around the world.

How We Make Our Relationship Last

What makes it last is our commitment to each other. We sought a counselor who helped us learn how to work with our different personalities and learn how they can complement each other. Before in our disagreements, we used to clash and pick each other apart. We have learned how to improve our communication, which comes in particularly handy in the middle of the ocean when we are miles away from anywhere.

We were ready for a big change in our lives and had been saving and planning for something like this for years. We don't focus on how to make it last but rather how to make it right for both of us.

Throw Caution to the Wind

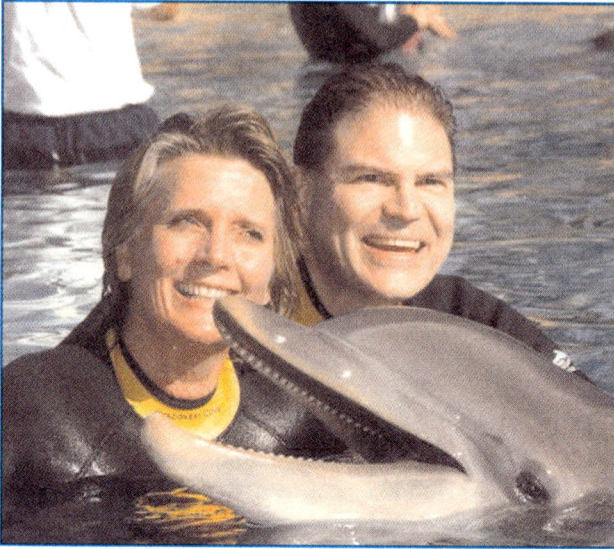

"The best relationships aren't 50-50. They involve each participant giving 80 percent while expecting 20; the magic is in the overlap."

Seasoned Love
Laura and Cole, North Dakota

*M*y first wife died in December 2000 of pancreatic cancer. She was only 50 years old and had been diagnosed just one month earlier. I loved and missed her immensely but I knew that my definition of happiness did not include a solitary life. Our two children were grown and though I enjoyed my space and privacy, I realized that I still had love to share.

Six months later, I had just concluded lunch with a friend at a local restaurant in Fargo, North Dakota. Due to the location of our seats and the layout of the restaurant, there were three different paths I could have used to exit the building. One was through the smoking section. Like many ex-smokers, I am sensitive to cigarette smoke, so I almost always avoid that section.

Strangely enough, on that day I decided to leave the building via the smoking section. I was halfway to the door when I passed a friend, Jan, who was having lunch with another woman. Non-smokers both, they were seated at a table in the smoking section because it was the only one that had been available when they'd arrived. Jan stood up and beckoned me over enthusiastically, inviting me to sit down. She is the head of an area foundation and a great networker.

I recognized Laura, her luncheon companion. We knew each other vaguely through our involvement in community projects. I joined them and the three of us began discussing various events in our lives.

I had just returned from a trip to Europe during which I had dispatched a series of e-mails to a list of friends, including Jan. The e-mails were of a humorous nature, relating my experiences on a rather whirlwind dash through Italy and France. Jan mentioned how funny they were and I found

myself offering to send copies to Laura. During the conversation, I told Jan and Laura that I had just been on my first date in thirty years, while attending a trade show in Florida. I confessed that I was just starting to date again, following Diane's death.

As the three of us talked (it was mostly Laura and I doing the talking), out of the corner of my eye I noticed that Jan was beaming. I began to suspect that her invitation had been more than just a friendly gesture. We all had a great time chatting but soon had to return to our respective jobs. On the way back to work, I called Jan on my cell phone and said, "You were trying to set us up, weren't you?"

"Yes!" she answered. "I've been trying to get you two into the same room for a month and you just happened to walk by." I decided to call Laura after I hung up with Jan.

"Did you happen to notice Jan with this big Cheshire Cat grin on her face?" I asked when Laura answered the phone.

"Yes," she said, "I thought she probably wanted us to volunteer for some project." I replied, "Well, she did...just not the type of project you were picturing." I asked if she was in a "dating mode," and whether she'd like to go to a movie that weekend. She accepted. We made plans to get together on Sunday evening.

Seasoned Love

By our third date, we both felt that we wanted to pursue this new relationship to see where it would go. We soon discovered that we were falling in love. Our times together have been some of the happiest of our lives.

When I met Laura she had been divorced for about two years and had three sons, the youngest of whom was seventeen and still lived at home. Two of her three boys were about the same age as my son and daughter. We've been fortunate in that our children have bonded like blood relatives.

Shortly before Laura and I were engaged, I found a small plaque while traveling with my daughter in Ireland. The quote on the back said, "Emerson's Law of Spiritual Gravitation: 'People destined to meet will do so, apparently by chance, at precisely the right moment.' C. G. Jung called this synchronicity." I bought two of the plaques, one for each of us.

How We Make Our Relationship Last

While we have divergent tastes in many things, we also share many views, and are completely committed to each other. Our relationship is colored by our ages as well as the losses that we both experienced. We frequently say that love is wasted on the young; they don't have the experience to appreciate the warmth, closeness, and reassurances that love in later life can bring.

We have yet to have our first fight or even a spat. Before we married, I mentioned this fact to a psychologist friend of mine. I had assumed that people were supposed to fight without hurting each other—that the occasional fight was normal and even healthy. She replied that many couples never argue because they refuse to let their disagreements progress to the confrontation stage. Their mutual respect is so strong and their communication is at such a deep level that they accept each other completely and discuss problems before any disagreement escalates. Laura and I are that way.

Having had previous relationships and having suffered the loss of love in different ways, we value each other and are certain that we were meant to be together. We laugh at many of the same things. Once at a Hot-air Balloon Festival we were part of a mass ascension of several hundred balloons. When we were in the air and awestruck at the beauty of the other balloons in the sunrise, Laura turned to me, put on a whiny voice and said, "You never take me anywhere fun!"

Despite our many adventures, some of our happiest moments have been spent lying in each other's embrace, just talking and sharing our feelings.

While sex is wonderful and fun, we have learned that intimacy is much more important. A great marriage isn't give and take—it's all give. It requires that both people give completely to each other. It's such a fantastic feeling to know that my wife adores me and that she knows the sentiment is returned in kind. A friend of mine once told me that the best relationships aren't fifty-fity. They involve each participant giving eighty percent while expecting twenty; the magic is in the overlap. I now know what he means.

Seasoned Love

"Why would such a handsome man want to go out with a mommy like me?"

Lost Dog

Judy and Ron, Virginia

One Saturday afternoon in November, while driving back from the hardware store, I noticed a beautiful black lab wandering around in a convenience store parking lot. Concerned for the dog's safety, I stopped and called it over to my truck.

The dog was a large male, very friendly, but collarless. He had obviously been swimming in the river nearby—all of the hair on his stomach was covered with ice. After asking several people in the parking lot if they knew who the dog's owner was, I decided he was lost. I coaxed him into my truck, then ran inside of the store and gave my name and phone number to the employee at the cash register, explaining to him that I was taking the dog home and would try to locate its owner.

Back at the truck, I noticed that the dog seemed very comfortable in the front seat of my truck and was taking a nap. Wow, I thought. Now what?

As I slowly drove up the hill to my house, I called my two boys at home and instructed them to put our dogs in the basement because I had a surprise for them. When I pulled into the driveway, I found them both waiting with their hands on their hips. They said in tandem, "Mom, we sent you to the hardware store, not to pick up a dog!"

My first plan was to check with the weekly newspaper (where I worked as an ad rep) the following day. No ads for a lost dog had been run that week. The daily paper, however, featured three ads for missing dogs, and I called them all. No one answered at any of the numbers listed, but I was able to leave messages at all three. I continued my Sunday as normal, still trying to figure out what to do with the dog (whom we had by now christened "Albert").

As I was preparing lunch, the phone rang. The man on the other end said "Hi, I'm Ron returning your call regarding the missing dog." I described Albert to him and he described his missing dog to me; neither of us thought it was a match, but figured it was worth a try.

Ron was not even from this area—he was working as a superintendent with a construction company in a nearby town. His dog traveled with him, and had disappeared on October 31. I gave him directions to my home, and began preparing the boys for the possibility that they'd have to part with a dog to which they had become attached.

Albert was wandering around in the kitchen, checking out the menu, when Maggie and Dane (my dogs) started barking to alert us that someone had arrived. As Ron climbed out of his truck, I let Albert out of the house. Ron knew immediately that Albert was not his dog. After a long conversation, we agreed that Ron would take the dog until I could find its owner. We exchanged phone numbers, and he put Albert into his truck.

I kept in touch with Ron every week to inform him that no one had come forward to claim Albert. Finally, I let him know that as far as I was concerned he could just keep the dog.

At the time, I was working in the next town over from Ron's job-site. Occasionally, I'd stop by to check in on Ron and Albert. (Actually, by this time I was more interested in Ron.) On December 28, I stopped by as usual, only to learn that Albert had vanished from the job-site. Ron searched everywhere, but to no avail.

I felt terrible for Ron, but could think of nothing that I could do to help him cope with the loss of a second dog in three months! As we talked, he mentioned that he'd like to take me out for dinner that night. I was shocked. Why would such a handsome man want to go out with a mommy like me? I had been divorced for ten years, and had decided that I was rotten at relationships because I always put my kids first. If a relationship caused problems with my kids, the guy would have to go. I agreed to have dinner with Ron, and drove home on cloud nine that afternoon.

After squeezing into my best jeans, fixing my hair, and splashing on perfume that I never used, I headed back to town to spend the evening with a man whom I really did not know. I'd agreed to meet him in the parking lot of a local restaurant. Nervous as hell, I smoked most of a pack of cigarettes on the way there. Upon parking my truck in the back of the restaurant, I noticed that his truck was parked nearby, but I didn't see Ron. I called him on my cell phone and he walked around the parking lot searching for me. All of a sudden, he appeared—a beautiful hunk of a man with a brown sports jacket and cowboy boots.

It was clear that Ron was as nervous as I was, because he stepped into the restaurant and immediately bellied up to the bar. We both ordered a beer and began to talk. To this day I could not tell you what we talked about, but neither of us smoked a cigarette until an hour later, when I finally broke down and asked, "Do you mind if I smoke?"

"Thank God," he said, as he pulled out his lighter and lit my cigarette. The ice broken, we moved over to a table and ordered dinner. We talked and talked, about everything and nothing.

The next thing I remember is walking into my living room and finding both boys waiting up for me. Several weeks later, I cautiously told them that I had been meeting Ron occasionally, and that I would like to invite him to our home for dinner so they could meet him.

"The dog man?" they asked.

Ron and I married after three years together.

Ron has one grown child who lives with his mother in another state. My kids grew up to consider Ron as their father. We all labor very hard to make our blended family work, with the help of Otis and Maggie, our two dogs.

How We Make Our Relationship Last

The one thing I find that helps us make it through the rough times is that we have fun together. Ron and I actually enjoy each other's company, as friends and coworkers as well as lovers. We make both inconsequential and important decisions together.

We also own a hotdog cart that we bought to supplement my income when I quit my full-time job. We sell hotdogs at private parties, family gatherings, and local auctions. We have a blast doing this. Sometimes we make money and sometimes we break even, but either way we have fun.

So my best advice is "play" frequently. Ron was married twice previously and I was married once, so neither of us wanted another divorce. We maintain honesty and always find time for each other.

"I tried everything. I was ready to give up and turn my dating life into a novel á la Bridget Jones' Diary."

My Own Backyard
Bill and Lisa, North Carolina

I was thirty-four and had been divorced for four years—long enough to work myself to a top career position, learn some lessons, and become acutely attuned to my biological clock.

At the time I was living in Holly Springs, North Carolina, a small town outside of Raleigh. I'd selected Holly Springs because I could afford to buy a house with a larger-than-postage-stamp sized lot and enjoy the safety of cul-de-sac living. But it was also a single woman's death wish. The women of Sex and the City don't have it nearly as tough as women of Single in the Suburbs. All of my friends were married with kids and all their friends were married with kids. I was telecommuting from my home, and in my career "engaging with others" meant interacting with ex-Department of Defense career-men in their fifties or sixties. In short, Prince Charming was unlikely to show up on my doorstep.

So I went after him. I decided to pursue love in the same manner I had pursued my grant-writing career goals: I was proactive, directed, and aggressive. I tried Internet dating, speed dating, volunteering, tarot card reading, feng shui, and old-fashioned wish-making (my sister having told me to write in pencil all my wishes under a full moon, then burn the list under the new moon).

While some of these activities produced entertaining dates—one man dropped his pants in the parking lot of a restaurant ostensibly to show me his tan lines—none of them yielded The One. I was ready to give up and turn my dating life into a novel á la Bridget Jones' Diary.

Then one day, I was just going about my daily routine, walking my dog in the local park, when I struck up a conversation with another dog owner taking the same route. Bill was new in town. He'd moved to Holly Springs from San Francisco because he wanted to try life in the country.

Our first date was on my thirty-fifth birthday. By our second date, we knew we were in love. There was a certainty that we both felt. Within one month, we were living together; within four months, we were married. As fairy-tale as it sounds, I had met my Prince Charming—he had all but shown up on my doorstep!

Soon after we married, we opened a personal matchmaking service to help other singles find love. After examining the trials and tribulations of our own dating lives, we decided to develop a business that addresses the challenges of being single at thirty-something, forty-something—even sixty- or seventy-something.

How We Make Our Relationship Last

Our clients and friends shake their heads at the fact that we took on so much in our first year: marriage, moving (I sold my house and moved into his), leaving our corporate jobs, and starting a new business. But we love it. We are very much alike, both Type A personalities who thrive on being the best. We love that we're working toward the same goal. Our business skills complement each other perfectly. Yes, it's been difficult, but we get through it because one of us always carries the other, we respect each other, and because we laugh so much together.

We are as conscious about scheduling personal time as we are about achieving our business goals. We constantly tell each other, "We rock!" We establish and maintain strict boundaries—for example, no talking about

My Own Backyard

business in the bedroom or on a Saturday night date. Keeping our romance alive is also very important to us. We leave each other love notes, dance in the kitchen, and tell each other how much we love each other and why. Every night as he goes to sleep, Bill whispers in my ear how much he respects and admires me.

Maintaining that "love glow" happens to be good for the business, but most importantly, we have built our business in such a way that it has been good for our relationship.

"We were orphans together. We know how lucky we are and will take care of each other always."

The Lucky Ones
Ly and Bun, Cambodia

Our story of love is simple. What brought us together in 1979, however, is anything but.

As a youth in Cambodia during the reign of the Khmer Rouge, I'd been forced from the city to work the rice fields. The Khmer Rouge was a communist regime run by Pol Pot, a dictator who believed education and urbanization were evil. Pol Pot evacuated the cities, forced people to do nothing but till the soil for nearly four years, and killed more than two million Cambodians.

Years later I overheard a conversation about a camp on the border of Thailand and Cambodia where I could be safe. As soon as the Vietnamese invaded Cambodia in December 1979, we all fled for our lives.

A friend of mine and I were fortunate to have found a pair of rickety old bikes that barely made it through mile after mile of uneven dirt roads, slippery streams, tons of dust, and excruciating heat for two seemingly endless days and nights. We arrived parched with thirst, weakened by lack of food, but alive. After nearly fours years of near-starvation while working in the rice fields, we were the lucky ones.

My English was rusty but I was immediately put to work at the camp as interpreter for a guy whose job it was to reunite families that had been separated by Pol Pot's regime. Conditions were meager and life was tough, but I was getting stronger each day.

Bun Chan Tha was working at the refugee camp as a nurse, delivering babies and dressing wounds, when her friend, Mrs. Pon, invited her to live in a spare bedroom.

I slept in a hammock in a small hut until Mrs. Pon also invited me to stay in her home. Bun Chan Tha and I were both so busy working that we only saw each other at dinnertime after long, draining days. Over meal after meal, we slowly discovered the many parallels in our lives. We had both lost our fathers to the Khmer Rouge. We had miraculously survived working in the fields. We were both orphans. Within six or seven months, we fell in love.

Two years later, the Vietnamese attacked our refugee camp. We managed to escape and run to the next camp. Our first child was six days old when we escaped to another camp in 1983. All in all, we spent over a decade together running from one refugee camp after another before the Vietnamese army departed our country and we returned to Cambodia.

The Cambodian government was now offering each returning citizen a small parcel of land or twenty dollars per person. A few weeks after pitching our first tent on our new land, masked robbers attacked us. Once again we were on the run, but we had each other and our family to care for. We eventually found a tent village. After years of living hand to mouth there, we were finally able to purchase another plot of land. I continued my interpreting. (By this time I spoke five languages.)

Bun Chan was the business-minded one between us. She managed the household and all of our money. Every year she bought and stockpiled wood. When we had enough money to hire builders, she orchestrated all the fiscal matters while I designed our first traditional Cambodian home, where we live today. The last of our eight children were born in 1998.

How We Make Our Relationship Last

What makes our relationship last is our love for each other, and the history we share. We lost so much at an early age. We were orphans together. We know how lucky we are and will take care of each other always. Each of our children will speak multiple languages. No fight or disagreement can compare to what we have been through in life. We are the lucky ones.

"I was stunned. I thought: he's probably married, with three kids and a station wagon!"

Can't Hide from Love
Lindsay and Dorwin, California

*I*n 1975, my sister was visiting San Francisco from London when she met a man named Dorwin, who mentioned he was going to New Zealand on holiday in a month. I was living in New Zealand, so she gave him my phone number and suggested that he call me if he needed a place to stay.

A month later, out of the blue, I got a call from the airport. A very lovely American-accented bloke introduced himself as Dorwin and explained the situation. Naturally, I said he could stay for a few days. He arrived half an hour later.

As soon as I opened my front door, my heart sort of leapt. Dorwin was buff and tanned, with long blond hair in a ponytail. He was wearing a lovely woven headband, leather shorts, and sandals. (What can I say—it was the '70s.) I too had long hair to my waist, and was equally hippyish in my long skirt and Indian shirt.

Right from the beginning, Dorwin was easy to talk to. We clicked immediately. The attraction was obvious. The only problem was that I happened to be engaged to a guy who had gone to work in Zimbabwe for a year. I had been infatuated with my fiancé and knew I had to wait for him...but

Dorwin and I spent two weeks together having a great time. He had his pilot's license so we rented a plane and flew around New Zealand's North Island seeing the sights. I really enjoyed his company. And then he left.

My fiancé returned and I married him six months later. But it wasn't a stable or happy relationship from day one.

Eighteen months passed before Dorwin returned for another holiday. I didn't admit it, but I was really sad to see him while I was so unhappily married. After a few awkward days, Dorwin left to travel the South Island. That was the last time I saw him for many years.

A few months later my husband and I moved to Sydney, Australia—a lame attempt to resuscitate our relationship. Why I thought the move would help, I have no idea! It didn't. Our relationship went from bad to worse. But, in contrast, the business we started together thrived. After a few years of emotional upheaval, we tried moving again, this time to Queensland, Australia, a "Surfers Paradise." Our relationship was anything but paradise. So, to make a long story shorter, after nine years of failed attempts to fix our marriage we called it quits. I returned to New Zealand to begin anew with my daughter.

I decided not to date for several years. My career was booming and I liked being independent and free. Eventually, however, I felt ready to jump back into the dating pool. During 1994, I dated several men; none of the relationships lasted long. By now, I really knew what I did and didn't want.

One day, while noodling on my computer, I came across a "people finder" website. I plugged in Dorwin's name and a second later the site popped up with his address and telephone number. I was stunned. I thought, he's probably married, with three kids and a station wagon! But I wanted to be sure so I decided to write him a note. I bought a beautiful card and wrote a brief note asking if he remembered me (it had been more than twenty years, after all!). I put my e-mail address at the bottom and posted it in September 1996.

A week later, I got an e-mail back from him. It started off, "Damn, can't hide anywhere!" He went on to tell me that he wasn't married, and explained what he'd been doing. I was ecstatic, and I thought he was so funny. We e-mailed back and forth. I had planned to go to London for Christmas, so we decided that I should stop by on my way back (I was traveling via Los Angeles) so that we could get together for a reunion.

Can't Hide from Love

The three weeks I spent in London were a blur because I was so excited about my upcoming meeting with Dorwin. I wondered how I was going to recognize him. Should we shake hands when we first met? What would he be like now?

On New Years' Day 1997, I stepped off the plane thoroughly jetlagged. I'd been diverted via Boston, so had already gone through customs and immigration when Dorwin caught me by surprise at the luggage carousel. All of a sudden I felt a tap on my shoulder, and when I turned around found myself enveloped in the biggest bear hug of all time.

We drove back to Dorwin's house, chatting easily. I found myself telling him things I never tell anyone but my closest friends. He was equally open and honest. I met his friends and family, all of whom were shocked that this confirmed bachelor had a lady staying at his place.

On day four, as we were driving up to visit his friends at Lake Tahoe, we decided to get married! We acknowledged the fact that we didn't love each other yet, but we knew that we had plenty in common. We also shared both a strong attraction and the maturity necessary to work out kinks as they came along—and that's what we've done.

It's been rocky in patches. Dorwin's dad and best friend both died the first year we were together. And for me, having to adjust to living in another new country was also tough.

How We Make Our Relationship Last

Dorwin says he has worked to make our relationship last by being patient and flexible. He thinks the fact that he is a Type B personality, whereas I am a Type A, goes a long way toward keeping our relationship interesting and lively. There is a subtle balance.

As for me, I think our relationship has lasted because I trust and respect Dorwin one hundred percent. And he keeps me grounded. He is my rock. He is super wise in a very quiet way. He has a small ego and large heart. And I know he truly loves me. He once told me that he would die for me. There wasn't any fanfare or drama involved, just a matter-of-fact statement. And because I trust this man implicitly, I know it's true. That, to me, is a rare and special love.

Can't Hide from Love

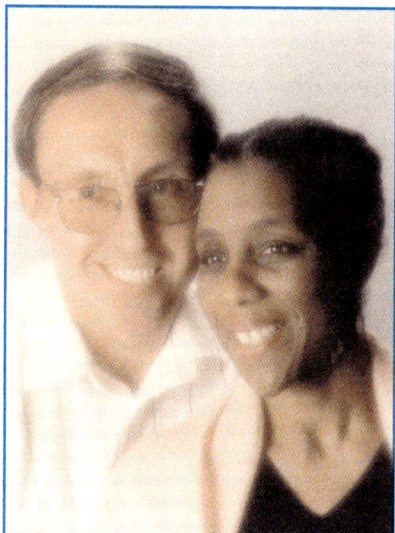

"Rather than making issues, we make space for one another."

Roller Skate Surprise

Pat and Rick, California

*I*n the summer of 1982, after five years of rigorous training as a rower, I was admitted to grad school at Berkeley. It was finally time to pursue a career and take a break from hard-core training. But before my sweat even had a chance to dry, I received a call from a coxswain.

"Hey Pat, there is a group of ex-Naval Academy rowers in town aching to row tomorrow and we need one more person. Can we count on you?"

I thought, Could my vacation from rowing vanish so soon? On the other hand, I know the pain of scouting out just one more rower…

The next morning at 6 a.m., I was greeted by handshakes all around and a "What's shaking?" from one of the strapping lieutenants of the USS Enterprise. We introduced ourselves as Pat and Rick, and we've been in the same boat ever since.

The row was dashing and swift, and we "connected," as they say. Two days later Rick invited a friend and me onto the USS Enterprise to watch the lunar eclipse. I was smitten. We toured the ship. I was fascinated, not so much with the combat elements, but with the technical aspects… and with Rick's polite demeanor.

Our first off-shore date was dinner at the house Rick shared with some shipmates. I arrived on roller skates—my customary mode of travel. Rick was impressed and embarrassed, exclaiming, "I should have offered you a ride!"

The convergence of my Berkeley ways and Rick's brand of thoughtful protocol kept us navigating new waters together. We could talk about anything, and often did, for hours. Once we ended up on the subject of the Navy providing diversity training. And there we were, an African-American Berkeley grad student and a white Navy grad, very comfortably discussing our upbringings, challenges, hopes, and dreams. My preconceptions about the Navy were being slowly altered by this charmer.

Our conversations, via letters and care packages, lasted well into Rick's nine-month deployment. Rick has saved every letter. Upon his return, he moved down to San Diego. I was training for the 1983 World Championships and continuing grad school. I flew down to visit as often as I could and we were still together when I made the team.

I was able to follow Rick to San Diego after winning a silver at the World Championships. After training with friends in San Diego for the 1984 Olympics, I headed to Boston and made the U.S. Olympic Team.

Sometime after the Olympics and a glorious Hawaiian vacation spent visiting Rick on deployment, I hinted at marriage, and we both celebrated by saying "yes."

Relatives on both sides were not quite ready for our union, but we were, and our relationship's success has shattered multicultural preconceptions to show that love transcends fears and fallibilities.

How We Make Our Relationship Last

What makes our love last is our core appreciation for one another, intertwined with a deep-rooted love. We don't argue over small things. I'm more liberal, he's more conservative. Our most heated discussions involve our different approaches to child rearing. My family was frank and direct in any discussion. His family was more restrained. Rick has taught me to be more sensitive about phrasing my constructive feedback. We've learned to balance "together time" with time spent following individual pursuits.

Roller Skate Surprise

Rick is the ultimate dedicated father and the quintessential loving husband. We've made the intimacy adjustments that many mid-fortyish couples make when romantic energy is consumed by the ravages of work and parenting. Our mundane chores have replaced some of the sexual excitement, engendering a more muted "gaze and talk" attitude. But we find balance.

For us, money has never been an issue. We're not big spenders, and when it comes to anything over $1,000, we always consult with one another.

Our kids are eleven, fifteen, and seventeen. They're dreams come true. But I remember Rick and I feeling liberated and gaining a new freshness when we could simply go on walks together and leave them at home. Teen years are tough. We are back to discussing how to approach parenting so that neither one of us feels that our core values are cast aside in the effort to keep three teens on course. We uphold a clear code of ethics: no swearing or hitting. We've maintained an unwavering respect for and an awe of one another through all these years. The longer we're married, the more peaceful is our rhythm. Rather than making issues, we make space for one another.

Last June 15, Rick woke me by saying, "We met twenty years ago to the day!" I was so impressed he remembered—he's still as charming and sweet as the day we met. To celebrate, he pulled out our letters and we read them to one another.

Roller Skate Surprise

"Trust and compassion. The trust grows with time and patience. The compassion supplies the patience."

Working Up the Nerve

Mark and Neil, New York

Neil: I met Mark as I was heading to my parents' home to come out of the closet. I knew that my mother would be upset, but willing to find a way to deal with the news and I thought that a book on the subject might be helpful. I went to A Different Light bookstore (a prominent gay and lesbian bookshop in New York), where I had already found many books that had helped me cope with being gay. When I got there, though I knew which book I wanted (*Are You Still My Mother?*), I was so anxious and distracted that I couldn't find it. I asked the bookstore clerk—this tall, blue-eyed guy with long blond hair and the kind of upper lip that always makes me kind of crazy—to help me. Then I headed off to the train.

Later that week, a pal who was acting as a mentor for me as I gradually started to explore gay life said, "Hey, did you see the new blond bookstore clerk at A Different Light? REALLY cute!" I thought back and remembered that, indeed, he really was cute.

At that point, I had never really dated anyone. I'd barely chatted with another guy, even during the few times I had gone to a gay bar or club with my friend. But that bookstore clerk…something about him…

Two months later, I was house-sitting for a former med school professor while he and his wife toured France. Their home was a magnificent duplex garden apartment in the West Village, complete with fig tree, wine cellar, and high maintenance cat. I was set! I had come out to my parents and now was going to be living in the heart of the West Village!

It was time to find a boyfriend. Multiple plans sprang to mind. I decided that on Wednesday I would go back to the bookstore and special-order a book from that cute clerk, making sure to give him my home number and let him know that I'd be in the neighborhood for the next few weeks.

Mark: The first time I remember seeing Neil was when he came in to order a book. He told me that he was going to be house-sitting around the corner from the store. He was very chatty, and while he was making the order he made sure that I had all his phone numbers and other crucial info.

Neil: After walking into the store, I set my plan into action. He was so handsome! Dashing, even! I did my best to make small talk, but felt shy about displaying interest in a guy. Then I ordered the book. While he was taking down the information, I noticed he had a silver band on his "wedding ring" finger. I didn't know what that meant, but my heart sank a little. Could he already have a boyfriend—one with whom he had exchanged rings? Nonetheless, my plan had its own momentum. I gave him my home phone number and address and then added my local number, telling him that for the next few weeks I'd be just around the corner. I left, excited, confused, and anxious. What should I do next?

Mark: That Saturday he came back to the bookstore, looking for "something to read." We chatted for an hour and he bought all three books that I recommended, which in retrospect were all really grim, intense, dark novels. But, hey, we were in our twenties, and those were the books that had really made an impact on me. What had also made an impact on me was that this cute, nerdy, boyish, Jewish doctor-in-training wanted badly to ask me out, but was clearly too afraid to do so. After he made his purchase and left the store, I went out after him. I followed him up the block until he got to West 11th Street (where he was staying). I would have felt foolish running up to him as if I was trying to catch him (although that was precisely what I wanted to do). Instead, I watched from a distance and pondered this stranger who had walked into my life.

Neil: On Saturday morning I was itching to know what was going on with the bookstore clerk. I knew I should give him time to call, but I couldn't stand waiting. Finally, about one o'clock in the afternoon, I walked the few blocks to the store. It was a lovely warm spring day, sunny, with the smell of fresh new foliage everywhere.

It wasn't easy to go in. Again, there was that dreadful shyness. But I was desperate to finally get my life moving, so I persevered. He smiled when he saw me. I reiterated that I was living in the neighborhood, and then asked for another literary recommendation.

We began talking. He told me about his current favorite books. It didn't matter what he recommended; he and his favorite books all seemed so arty and sophisticated. I could see that the other clerks were throwing glances at us, amused at the flirt-fest that was going on, and only slightly annoyed that he was leaving them to deal with the rest of the customers on a busy afternoon. Finally, after an hour, I chose three of Mark's recommendations and purchased them.

Now I had something of his in my hands. It was an intimate feeling, carrying books that meant something to him and that he had shared with me. I went back to my temporary, luxurious home. I immediately began reading one of the books, falling back on the bed, thoroughly happy. It felt like my life had finally started.

Mark: When I got back to the store I looked up his Special Order form and called him. The conversation went something like this:

"Hi. Neil?"

"Oh, Mark! Hi!"

"Yes. I'm surprised you recognized my voice. Listen, I was just wondering, do pathologists drink beer?"

Working Up the Nerve

He was so happy to hear from me that he said "yes" (kind of a lie, since he really didn't drink alcohol at all). We made a date for that night.

Neil: I found myself waiting on the steps of the brownstone a full half-hour before he got off work. I was beside myself. I stared fixedly at that end of the block, and when he appeared my heart leapt. But I stayed put. I was trying so hard to be sophisticated and at ease, as though waiting for a date to pick me up was a common and natural occurrence. In fact, I'd never been picked up for a date before. So I sat there, ready to leap out of my skin until he reached the steps.

Mark: Within a month, we had moved in together. That was seventeen years ago.

How We Make Our Relationship Last (*Neil's version*)

As Mark once noted, "Trust and compassion." The trust grows with time and patience. The compassion supplies the patience, and (for us) was there from the beginning. It was what attracted me to Mark in the first place. It continues to make him my favorite person. (That and the fact that he still thinks I'm cute.) We allow ourselves to change; we even encourage it. We've both shed many skins over the years, and when those raw, difficult transitions were happening, each of us stood by the other, waited, witnessed, and cheered.

How We Make Our Relationship Last (*Mark's version*)

It's as simple as just choosing to stay. So many people run at the first sign of difficulty. Certainly, my knee-jerk response to many problems in life is to run away. But when you decide to stay and make the relationship work, then at least you are giving it a fighting chance. When you run away, there is only one possible outcome. It has always seemed to me that after years of being in a relationship, you wind up having so much invested in the other person…do you really want to start all over again? Is it really worth it? There must be a way to figure out whatever it is that is causing a problem and work through it, together.

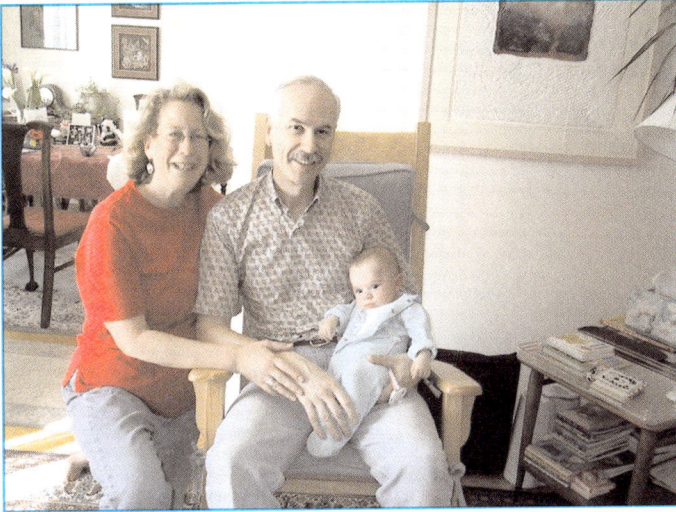

"I knew I needed to find someone very different from myself. I wanted to have a chance to explore someone else's world."

Someone Different
Rori and Allan, California

We'd both quit our jobs, lived six thousand miles apart, had never met, and had independently made plans to backpack around Southeast Asia.

Our first meeting was brief and insignificant. We were staying in a guesthouse in Cameron Highlands (central Malaysia) and talked one night before heading off in different directions. About a week later, I was on a bus on Panang Island (northwest Malaysia) and felt a tap on the shoulder. There was Allan again, smiling, and then, two stops later, gone. I didn't even remember his name, but he remembered mine.

Another two weeks went by. I was in Bangkok, not having a very good time. I was homesick and overwhelmed by the size of the city and the pollution. During breakfast in the communal room one morning, Allan appeared again. Why this guesthouse? There were hundreds of guesthouses in this area of Bangkok. As he emerged from a tuk tuk (a three-wheeled, covered motorcycle), I was the first person he saw, sitting in the very guesthouse that had been recommended to him.

I was ready to see a familiar face. Allan and I accompanied each other for four days. Or perhaps I should say that we spent four days having a series of delightful misadventures—like frequently getting on the right bus, but going the wrong direction. On one memorable occasion in Chinatown, we ordered some orange juice, only to discover that salt had been generously sprinkled in that morning's batch instead of sugar. We had no way of explaining the problem in Thai, but we got the waitress to try a sip and she burst out laughing. This was but one of many truly unforgettable moments we shared together, and it was nice to have a friend.

I remember having a very strong intuitive sense that at some point I would see Allan again, although I had no idea when or how. He had traveled across the United States on a student visa, and had lived and worked in Santa Cruz over one summer in the 1970s. Santa Cruz isn't too far from my home, at least in West Coast terms. When we parted this time, we exchanged addresses.

I was on my way to Burma for seven days; Allan carried on to northern Thailand. On Allan's journey back from Chiang Mai, he struck up a conversation with fellow travelers who told him that they'd met an American woman named Rori who was on her way back from Burma. He asked, "How did her trip go?" When he returned home to England, he wrote to me, telling me he'd heard I'd had a great time in Burma.

The following year, I went with a girlfriend to the Fringe Theater Festival in Edinburgh, Scotland, and decided to contact Allan. That was when our romance began. The next year I did the same, but stayed longer. Allan's mother died very suddenly during this visit, and, having lost my father six years earlier, I was able to be a support to him through his loss. This experience contributed to the deeper connection that was developing between us. It was nice to be together, and tempting to think about our relationship becoming more than a transatlantic affair. Neither of us, however, could figure out where the relationship was going or what we wanted.

Over the next two years, Allan came to visit for three week-long holidays. These visits were friendly and fun, yet followed by a deep sadness each time he had to depart. We also shared long phone calls once or twice a week—something we both looked forward to—and we found it very hard to put the phone down. Our conversations flowed so easily. The closeness we shared (a strong part of our mutual attraction) was comforting.

In 1990, we took a trip to Mexico where, as a result of all the back-and-forth over four years, we decided to tone down our relationship. Allan owned his house in England, had a good job, and a close circle of friends; I had an apartment, a job that was going nowhere, and was tired of being single in San Francisco. We knew we were falling in love, but didn't want to admit it because the situation seemed impossible to resolve.

Well, if you want something badly enough, you'll find a way to make it happen. In October of 1990, Allan wrote to ask if I would consider moving to England. He said he was ready to open his heart and his home to me. I gave it a few months' thought. I knew that if I didn't accept his offer I would probably regret it for the rest of my life, and I couldn't live with that.

On March 9, 1991, I arrived in Britain. We had discussed the possibility of moving to San Francisco but never set a date. Even though my two years in Britain turned out to be a mixed bag, I knew that it was a good investment in someone with whom I deeply wanted to share my life.

In the spring of 1993, Allan got a job offer in San Francisco, which included moving expenses and a temporary apartment. Once again, the universe was smiling on us. A year later, we were married.

April 10, 2004 marked our tenth anniversary. We have just adopted a son and are very happy to finally be a family.

How We Make Our Relationship Last

I think of Allan as my "high-quality life partner." There was a thread that connected us from the beginning, and we met at the right time in our lives.

What works for our relationship is an abiding friendship and inherent trust. We challenge each other, and I've learned not to take myself too seriously. Even though we are from very different backgrounds, we share similar values. Allan said to me once, "I knew I needed to find someone very different from myself. I wanted to have a chance to explore someone else's world." We also laugh a lot, as Allan has a razor sharp British wit.

I think in a relationship you have to keep something for yourself, whether it is an activity, an interest, or time spent socializing with a set of friends. It helps to remind each of us that we are not just part of a couple, but individuals as well.

Much of our success was due to timing—you have to be receptive to love and open to opportunity.

Someone Different

"On August 19, 1981, we were married by a drunk Justice of the Peace who hollered for his blind receptionist to witness the five minutes it took to change our lives forever."

Drillin' for Love

Ike and Tim, Montana

In 1980, my friend Bobby hired me as the company clerk for an oil drilling company in Jeffrey City, Wyoming. I was recently divorced and living with my sons, ages one and two, and a malamute husky named Nikki. I was not looking for a relationship.

Soon after starting my new job, the manager gave me a phone number and told me in no uncertain terms, "Call this damn driller and tell him to get his fanny over to the office immediately." I called the driller and was surprised to hear a soft Texas drawl accompanied by good manners and a charming voice.

Around five that afternoon, the office door banged open and Tim's silhouette filled the doorway. There he stood, the tallest man I had ever seen, wearing an old straw cowboy hat, a blue denim shirt with torn sleeves, and mirrored sunglasses. (I hated not being able to see his eyes!) I was struck by an insane notion: "He's mine forever." Immediately, my rational mind took over and dismissed the idea.

Tim stepped through the door and said, "You must be Ike."

"You must be Tim," I replied.

That week, Tim tried every tactic to get me out on a date, but I refused. I was intrigued but he reeked of testosterone and I figured a man like that would only break my heart. Finally, I consented to a phone conversation. We talked on the phone for hours that night.

During the course of the conversation, we figured out that each of us had been trying to get the other fired. It turned out Tim was the guy I'd been refusing to pay because he'd been demanding his reimbursement in beer. I'd called Bobby to say he should fire the bum that wanted booze instead of cash. At the same time, Tim was calling Bobby and telling him to fire the witch that wouldn't pay him.

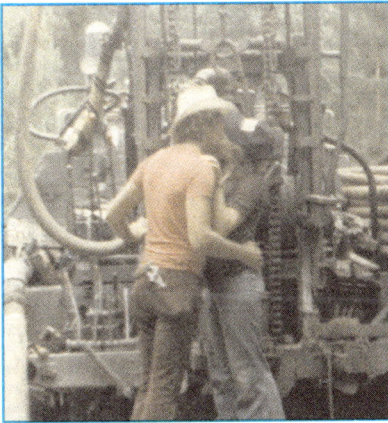

Then one afternoon, Tim unexpectedly stopped by to tell me he was leaving for Denver that night, and to ask if he could take Nikki with him. To this day, I have no idea why I let my dog go with someone I barely knew.

At 10 p.m., Tim parked his drilling rig in front of my bedroom window. His headlights flooded the room. He marched into the house, picked me up, held me tight, kissed me in the blinding lights of the rig, and then walked out the door with my dog.

Tim called me from Denver on New Year's Eve and asked me to take a chance on him. His next job was in Texas and he predicted I would go with him. I told him I wouldn't. But in January, when the crew headed for Texas, sure enough, I went.

It meant leaving office work behind and returning to the field, where I'd already worked as a survey hand, a welder's helper, an explosives handler, a head linesman, a truck driver, a crew supervisor, and a cable puller. Tim hired me as his drill helper. Together, Tim and I set a drilling footage record in Cotulla, Texas. When one client fired me for being female, it was Tim who rallied the other drill crews, convincing everyone to walk off the job until I was allowed back to work. He was my knight in shining armor—and he still had my dog.

Drillin' for Love

In August of that year, Tim took me to see his grandfather in Everman, Texas. His grandfather liked me, said I was the best thing for his grandson, and gave us his blessing. On August 19, 1981, we were married by a drunk Justice of the Peace who hollered for his blind receptionist to witness the five minutes it took to change our lives forever.

Tim and I have raised three children. He remained by my side when I joined the Navy at the ripe old age of twenty-five and when I lost my younger brother to a mountain in Tibet. We went to college together in 1990 and graduated together in 1995. We have traveled across the United States five times. In 1999, while both of us were still under 50, we became grandparents.

We've been together for twenty-four years and are still working as a team. When I joined the Navy, I asked Tim to let me support us both since he had supported me for so long. It can be hard for a working man to let his wife become the sole breadwinner, but I persuaded him by giving him an extra five hundred dollars a month to do with as he pleased, buying him a new V65 black motorcycle and a set of golf clubs, and kicking him out of the house every Thursday night for bonding with the guys. In return, I got breakfast in bed, and never had to wash a single item, clean, lift a rag, or cook. He put a sign on the front door to keep folks away so I could sleep in when I was working night shifts. Today, I'm an artist with a frame shop and Tim is my constructive art critic and moral supporter. When I'm not running my business, I run Tim's office. Tim spoils me.

How We Make Our Relationship Last

We have "debates" rather than fights. We talk to each other and respect each other's thoughts, even when they differ. Tim's a right-brain concrete thinker and I am in left field with a vivid imagination. I think my mom was right when she said that opposites attract. He's quiet and I'm loud. He's patient and I expect instant results. He taught me to play dominos; I lose at poker but whip him at chess. He's careful and I am a thrill seeker. I'm still trying to get him to jump out of an airplane!

Each of us works at making sure the other person is happy, and I guess that's the key. The happier Tim is, the happier I get. We have a very rich life, which I'm sure still holds wonders we have yet to discover.

What makes a good, lasting relationship depends upon the people involved and how hard they wish to work at creating what they want. A marriage is a wonderful "job" when you find the right person by accident.

Drillin' for Love

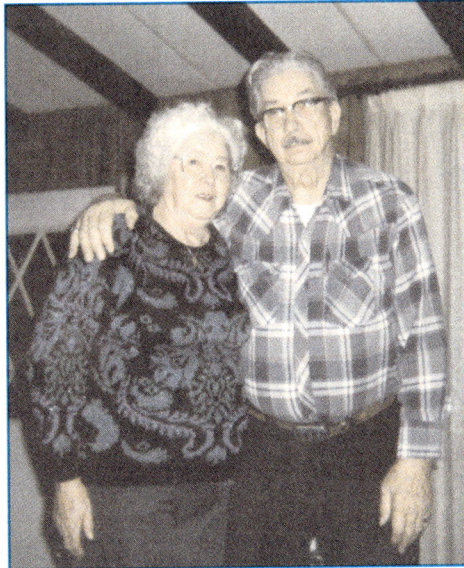

"After more than sixty-four years of marriage, I lost my sweetheart. I still speak to her—every evening I wish her good-night."

Million Dollar Love for Two Bucks

Fred and Florence, Oregon

When I first met my sweetheart-to-be, she was living across the street from my mother and me. My brother and his wife used to perform at a nightclub in Racine, Wisconsin. One night I asked my future wife to go dancing at the nightclub, and she accepted my invitation.

Eventually, I asked if she would consider marrying me. She said, "Maybe." Time went on, and I finally got the ok, so I purchased a diamond ring set (engagement and wedding band). I knew in my heart that she was my one and only, and that I was going to have her as my wife.

On March 20, 1937, we were married by the Justice of the Peace in Racine, Wisconsin. My brother and his wife were best man and bridesmaid.

After the ceremony was over, I inquired of the Justice of the Peace, "What's the charge?"

He replied, "What is she worth?"

I gave him a two-dollar bill and said, "Keep the change."

In September 2001, after more than sixty-four years of marriage, I lost my sweetheart. I still speak to her—every evening I wish her goodnight. I purchase her a rose for every holiday, and also for her birthday. We have five children, seven grandchildren, and thirty-four great-grandchildren.

How We Made Our Relationship Last

My only advice to couples is to keep in mind, "For better and for worse." Never forget your sweetheart. Also, remember that it takes two to tangle. If you have a spat or argument, be sure to kiss her and bid her good-night. I did this for sixty-four years. If you do these things, you will never visit divorce court.

I served in two wars and got through them to return to the one I love the best. I still love her. I am eighty-six years old. With love and god speed. Florence was the love of my life.

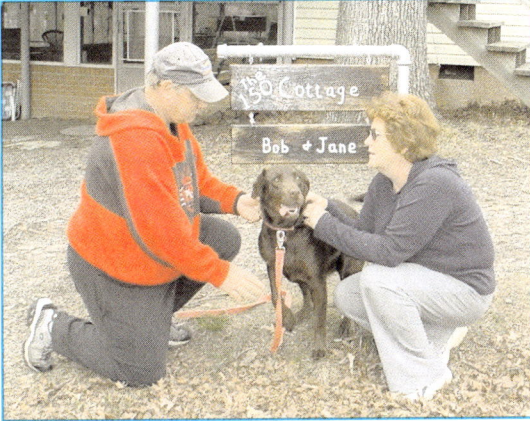

"We have agreed not to discuss things that are so important to us as individuals that they prompt button-pushing and identity-wounding."

A Gift from God

Jane and Bob, North Carolina

I'd just finished an adult Bible Study session and was waiting for my teenage children to finish their Youth Group project for the evening. Their activity that night was to write letters of support for the troops in Operation Desert Storm (since this was January 1991). Not having anything else pressing to do while I waited and, feeling somewhat patriotic, I decided to pen a letter myself.

The youth advisers had obtained envelopes addressed to "Any service member." I sat on a loveseat in the youth area and wrote a friendly, supportive letter. Since I knew that my letter could land in the hands of any soldier regardless of age or gender, the portion about myself was very generic. I reported that I was recently divorced and wrote about my three children, my career as a high school English teacher, and some of my interests. I tried to make the letter cheerful and interesting, while at the same time expressing my appreciation for the sacrifice that the service men and women were making during their tours of duty. When I finished writing the letter, I put it in the box with the others and promptly forgot about it.

At the time, I had been separated for four years and had not been asked out even once. My entire post-divorce romantic life consisted of a single (unsuccessful) blind date. Though I was busy with my job and with my children's activities, I was beginning to grow weary of not having a companion.

One Sunday evening in March, exhausted from the strain of raising my children alone, out of sheer frustration I uttered a prayer as I made my fourth nine-mile trip to church (I'd spent the day shuttling one or more of the children to church events). In the car alone, as I was returning to pick them up, I slammed my hands down on the steering wheel and prayed aloud, "God, if you intend for me to do this all by myself, I can surely do it, and I thank you sincerely for the strength to do it! I really do! But if you mean for me to have a partner for the rest of my life, just please, please show me a sign!"

That Thursday, in my mailbox, I found a letter from a sergeant in the United States Army! My hands trembled and my heart was pounding as I read the letter. It seemed that we had much in common. His wife was deceased and he had three daughters approximately the same age as my children. We shared the same interest in music and leisure activities. God had sent me the sign I had prayed for only days before!

Thus began an exchange of letters that led to our meeting, falling in love, and marrying in April of 1992. We now have a blended and growing family of six children, three children-in-law, and four grandchildren. Our children get along well, and my husband and I are enjoying the pleasures of our empty nest now that the children have homes and careers of their own.

A few months after we began our relationship, I asked my husband how the army distributed those mass mailings. He told me that when a mailing arrived the soldiers would just sort of stand around while someone disbursed the letters by location, calling out, "Anybody from North Carolina?" etc. He said that a "kid from Kentucky" took my letter and read it, then said to him, "Here, Sarge, I think this is for you."

He'd replied, "I don't have time for any letters like that."

The soldier from Kentucky said, "Well, I think you better read this one." The so-called "kid from Kentucky" had become God's agent, sending me a sign that I was not, after all, to spend the rest of my life alone.

A Gift from God

How We Make Our Relationship Last

Our relationship lasts for a number of reasons. First of all, having a blended family—the result of bringing together six children ranging in age from ten to nineteen (four girls, two boys)—certainly provided many opportunities for bonding and working together. We are very fortunate that our children's development as individuals and as siblings progressed relatively smoothly. There was, however, rarely a dull moment, and my husband and I faced many challenges.

Now that the children are adults out on their own, we have discovered that part of what sustains our relationship is that we complement one another in many ways. Politically, for example, one of us is slightly left of center and the other slightly right of center. One of us is a procrastinator and the other likes to strike while the iron is hot. One of us is better at seeing the "big picture" and pursuing a vision, while the other is more practical.

Our differences provide opportunities for lively and (mostly) playful "discussions" from time to time, especially concerning political and social issues. We have agreed, however, not to discuss things that are so important to us as individuals that they prompt button-pushing and identity-wounding. We do not discuss the army or teaching, because each of us thinks that the other is out of his/her element when crossing this boundary into the other's domain.

In addition to these two significant bonding agents, there are simpler things. We share similar tastes in music, entertainment, travel, leisure activities, food, and general pace of living.

A Gift from God

"Staying active and nurturing friendships keeps us young at heart."

Dovetailing on the Slopes
Mae Ling and Warren, California

When I first met Warren, he was sitting at the bottom of a hill on a snow-covered mountain, cursing and trying to get his skis back on. I offered him a dime to use as a tool to tighten his bindings. To his disbelief, it worked. The next time I saw him was at dinner that evening, mingling with friends from our singles' ski club.

We later found out we'd both been born in San Francisco, had each been partially raised in China, went to the same elementary school, and originally had the same last name—I say originally because Warren was a "Paper Son" (a child brought into the United States from China under purchased ID papers). "Paper" children took on new names and identities. Both of our families had roots in the Chinese laundry business.

Considering the similarities and parallels in our backgrounds, our paths could have crossed many times. Yet we might never have actually met if not for the Chinese Ski Club. For both of us, this club was our main form of weekend entertainment, a much-needed escape from long workdays.

After numerous ski trips—to Utah, Aspen, etc.—Warren ended up sitting in front of me on the bus headed to the ski lodge in Tahoe. From that trip forward we spent more and more time together, getting to know each other slowly as a couple. Neither of us had ever been married.

To this day we have an active social life. There is a group of seventeen couples with which we socialize on a weekly basis, and seven couples with whom we travel on vacations. We usually plan one trip outside of the United States and one in the United States (for the domestic vacation, we rent a van and drive). Staying active and nurturing friendships keeps us young at heart.

How We Make Our Relationship Last

Meeting each other half way is what makes our relationship work. Warren grew up in a family in which arguing was considered normal. He learned early on that I did not like to fight. I back off during arguments. He reminds himself not to shout in the heat of the moment, and not to say words that hurt. We offset each other in skill areas—where he is strong, I am weak, and vice versa. I keep track of the finances; he fixes and remodels the house. I keep saying no to expenses; he keeps saying yes.

Thirty-four years, two kids, two cats, several rabbits, birds, and a goldfish later, we are still happily married. Little did we know how far my original ten-cent investment would take us.

Dovetailing on the Slopes

"Communication can be a tight rope. I'm better able to find a balance with maturity and the passage of time."

A Powerful Force

Anne-Marie and Marcus, California

Sunday mass was my chance to see Marcus. At age ten, I was already interested in older men. Marcus was thirteen and he seemed so cool. Our families went to church every Sunday; unbeknownst to them, my biblical interest only went as far as hoping to catch a glimpse of Marcus when he bothered to attend.

Since my mom knew Marcus's mom, over the years we had occasion to talk. Our deep conversations went something like:

"Hi."

"Oh, hi. How ya doin'?"

"Fine, what about you?"

My heart would pound in my ears and my tongue always tied the minute he approached. There was no way for him to know that I had this massive crush on him.

Five years later, when I was fifteen (June 1, 1986), my girlfriend called and said, "You'd better sit down, Anne-Marie. Guess who just called to ask if you were dating anybody?" I just about jumped out of my skin with joy.

Because our moms were friends, my family made an exception to their must-be-16-to-date rule. I think they found it cute that the two of us were dating. When we got serious, they were not so thrilled. As a matter of fact, at one point they forbade us from seeing each other. Finally, they gave up and decreed that we could only see each other one night each weekend.

Needless to say, our parents were relieved the day we decided to take a break, leave St. Louis, and go to separate colleges. Marcus went to California and I to Indiana. Their relief lasted only two years—we started right back where we'd left off when we both returned from college. Marcus was still the only man I'd ever been interested in.

After much discussion (and maintaining a monogamous, committed relationship for more than eight years), we decided California was the natural place to pursue our careers together. My focus was marine biology and Marcus was a music major.

The institution of marriage never seemed important to us. We knew we were committed to each other and never thought a piece of paper was necessary. At least it never mattered until I was rushed to the emergency room. Marcus was not allowed to accompany me because he was neither my spouse nor a family member.

So, after eighteen years as a committed couple, we decided to make our relationship official. Not exactly the most romantic of reasons, I admit, but at least we had become a sanctioned couple in the eyes of society. It wasn't until we were married that we learned the significant power of marriage as a rite of passage. We were (and still are) shocked at the fact that our families never really considered our relationship a serious one until we were married, even though Marcus was the only man I'd ever kissed. We now recognize that marriage is a powerful force not to be taken lightly.

How We Make Our Relationship Last (*Anne-Marie's version*)

What keeps us together? Blocking the door when Marcus wants to leave will work... but seriously, we just don't argue about silly things. Maturity helps. We occasionally have a quick buildup and release and then the argument is over. He is my best friend as well as my husband.

We also take space to figure things out, rather than allowing disagreements to escalate. Lowering stress in our lives also helps.

How We Make Our Relationship Last (*Marcus' version*)

The qualities that make our relationship last may be unique to couples who meet at an early age. How many people find it easy to walk away from someone they've trusted and grown up with? Love is such a nebulous word, but friends are always friends. Unseen forces hold us together even through the tough times.

Communication can be a tightrope. I am better able to find a balance with maturity and the passage of time. I tend to try to anticipate potential arguments in order to figure out what Anne-Marie wants so that we can get back to an equilibrium. I ask myself what I'm willing to give up in order to achieve a mutually acceptable solution.

It also helps to surround yourselves with loving, good people.

A Powerful Force

"I never knew that such happiness was a possibility in this world. So many times I thought, this love is so big, this joy is so great, my heart is so full—how could one person be so blessed in this life?"

Untraditional Tradition

Sara and Dev, Pennsylvania

*D*ev: The first thing I noticed were her sneakers. Yellow Nikes with a blue swoosh. It was the beginning of a beautiful California summer at KlezKamp (a Yiddish music and culture camp in the Santa Cruz mountains—funny place for Klezmer music). I'd been there two days already, on work-study, with a crew of folks with whom I was having trouble finding much in common. She was in the registration line.

Something familiar about her captured my attention. Just as I was thinking that she reminded me of my cousin Michael, I heard her say to the registration person, "I know. I look like everyone's cousin Susan." Close enough. As a Jew living in northern California, it's easy to get excited when you see someone who looks like a member of the tribe: dark, thick, wavy hair; generous eyebrows; deep brown eyes; full lips; a smile that looks like home.

When I got to my cabin—the old camp kind, with a dozen bunks lined up in rows—I saw the Nikes again, this time all by themselves. I chose the bunk across from hers. She entered the cabin and introduced herself as Sara. Later, she offered to balance my trumpet on her chin. I was horrified. My trumpet was my most precious possession. At that time in my life, it was my best friend.

The next morning we met in clarinet class. Sara and I sat together on a bench in the sun, learning tunes and listening to the teacher, Margot, play. I have never in my life heard anything like Margot's clarinet—rich and full, laughing and weeping, dancing and mourning, and now a memorable part of that magical time in our lives.

Soon we were buddies. Over the course of five days at camp, we talked and talked, played music together in sacred spaces, and kept seeking each other out. Our connection was deep and solid, and made me feel alive to my core. Sara was smart and funny, thoughtful and creative, a good talker, a good listener, an easy partner in silence. One night, after hopping the fence into the pool for a late swim, we lay out on the dirt roadway, looking up at the stars and telling stories deep into the night.

We shared our love of Jewish music and our struggles over what it means to be Jewish in this world. We shared a commitment to political activism, and discovered that we had even been arrested together in a massive protest at the national nuclear weapons laboratory in Livermore.

After camp ended, we began talking on the phone every night for hours. Weeks later, when we finally saw each other again, we kissed, and I knew. I never thought I could love anyone as much as I love Sara. I never knew that such happiness was possible. So many times I've thought: this love is so big, this joy is so great, my heart is so full—how could one person be so blessed in this life?

Sara: When Dev walked into the cabin, I offered to balance her trumpet on my lips because I was taken with her and wanted to impress her with my vast knowledge of circus tricks. Perhaps it wasn't the best approach, but hey, I'm a circus artist. It's what I do. There was no trumpet teacher at camp, so Dev joined me in clarinet class. As we got to know each other, we often snuck off to play duets in the building that served as both a synagogue and holocaust memorial. The building was built into a hillside; through one set of windows, you could see the treetops and through the opposite set of windows, the tree trunks. In between these windows we sat and played music together, forging a link between past and future.

Dev wasn't just beautiful, interesting, smart, and sexy, but also (and this is crucial) incredibly funny in a way that touched my heart. During this amazing week spent connecting with Dev and shamelessly flirting (on my part), our romance soared to the soundtrack of the Klezmer music around us, to tunes filled with the joys and troubles of life. Four years after we met, we got married in the synagogue in the camp where we found each other. As Margot's clarinet lifted us into the air, we floated to the chuppah, the wedding canopy. We danced and we sang and soaked in all the love and the joy and goodness.

How We Make Our Relationship Last

We've been together for over fifteen years now. We have three basic rules for our relationship:

1) Everyone always gets what she wants. (This gives our relationship a sense of abundance rather than scarcity, and makes us seriously consider what we "want." Wanting what you know you'll get can be very different from wanting what you know you can't have.)

2) You don't have to do anything you don't want to do—unless the other person wants you to do it. A subset of this rule is the "birthday privilege." On your birthday, you get to pick what to do, what to eat, etc., and the other person has to not only go along for the ride, but also have a good time.

3) No one is allowed to be intentionally hurtful.

But wait, you say, these rules are full of contradictions! How can everyone always get what she wants? How can you be both exempt from doing what you don't want to do, and obligated to do what you don't want to do? Bingo! The beauty of our rules is that they remind us that relationships are not about rules. Really, we just need to think about what we need for ourselves, and what our partner needs, and always try to take care of each other with compassion and kindness.

(Since our son Jesse was born, rule number one has been amended to read, "Jesse always gets what he wants." We hope to repeal the amendment in the next decade or two.)

Untraditional Tradition

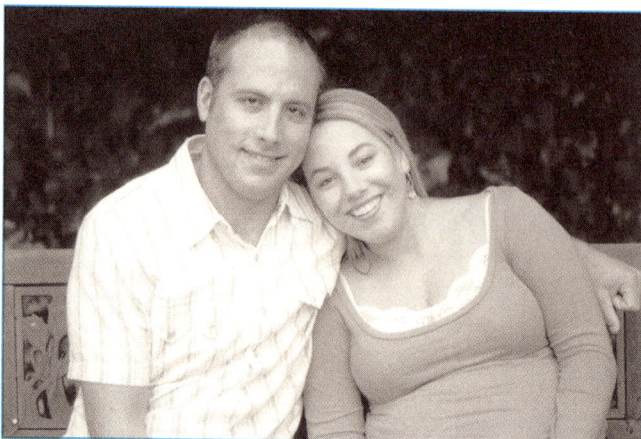

"When I get angry, I remember what an incredibly good person he is. Whatever the problem between us is, it will never outweigh that feeling."

The Greatest Cliche

Sasha and Ursula, California

I t was the greatest cliche moment of my life, right out of a trashy romance novel. I was at a huge party at the Maritime Hall in San Francisco. Above the crowd I saw Sasha; actually, what I saw were his eyes. My immediate thought was, "This is the man I'm going to marry."

What I didn't realize that night was that this was the same guy my friend Megan had been telling me she wanted me to meet. A couple of weeks later, she invited me to a small party at the home of a mutual friend. Shortly after we arrived, the doorbell rang. Inexplicably (since this wasn't my house), I jumped up and said, "I'll get it!" I opened the door and there were those eyes again.

The first time we danced together, he was DJing a party and during one of his breaks I approached him and simply asked, "So, when are you going to dance with me?" There were definitely sparks from the beginning, but it took awhile (well, at least several weeks) for our romance to burst into flames. I was enjoying the freedom of being nineteen, Sasha was shy, and we were always surrounded by friends.

Finally late one night, we took a walk alone to Duboce Park. It was raining gently and we sat on a bench and talked for hours. On the way home that night, we kissed for the first time. Seven years later, we were married.

How We Make Our Relationship Last

From the beginning, we got along like buddies. This probably says a lot about why our relationship works so well. Our friendship is key—that and that we have no doubt we're going to be together. "I can't imagine my life without her." Those are Sasha's words, but I feel the same way: I can't imagine living without him.

We do have our differences. He is reserved with his emotions and, even if I want to, I can't seem to hide what I'm feeling. He's cautious and deliberate about making decisions while I tend to act more quickly. He needs his time alone and I can be with people all the time. We have to make adjustments for our differences, especially now with the baby. But because we know we are together, if we can't come to an agreement, we figure we just have to get over it. When I get angry, I remember what an incredibly good person he is. Whatever the problem between us is, it will never outweigh that feeling.

The Greatest Cliche

"If I hadn't lived alone for those three years, done some 'inner work,' and learned more about who I was and what I wanted in life, I do not believe we would have met."

Inner Work

Sally and Dick, North Carolina

Sally: In 1977, following my divorce, I decided to move from New York to Arizona. My three children were grown and, though I remained friendly with my ex-husband, I had always dreamed of living in the Southwest. I sold my home in New York and designed and built an isolated house in the middle of the Tucson desert. My closest neighbor was over a mile away.

Being a gregarious soul, I met people easily and was soon besieged with friends' offers to set me up on blind dates. I refused, politely. I was living alone for the first time in my life and loving every minute of it. I adopted two stray wolf-dog hybrids; when the three of us went for long walks in the desert each morning, I thought I had died and gone to heaven.

I stayed busy taking classes, riding horseback up in the mountains, seeing friends, doing aerobics, and getting used to going home alone at night. For two years I found delight in my solitude and "knew" I would never marry again. I didn't even want to date!

However, after three years or so I began to think that it might be nice to have a "playmate" with whom to enjoy movies, weekend excursions, etc. I wasn't looking for a relationship, per se…just a male companion. I expressed this desire to my best friend and added, "I'm not in a hurry. I love being alone, but if you know someone really nice, I'm ready to meet him."

She told me that Dick, her husband's best friend, was separated from his wife and might want to meet me. I said, "Never mind. If he's not divorced already, I'm not interested."

However, on that very same day, Dick said to my friend's husband, "My wife and I have decided to get a divorce. If you know anyone nice for me to go out with, I'd like to meet her. I don't want a relationship…just someone to do things with."

My friend called me the next morning to report this very odd coincidence, and asked if she should give Dick my phone number. I replied that it would be easier if she would agree to have us both over to dinner one evening. (It would also be less awkward in case it turned out that we didn't like each other.)

We met at my friend's house for dinner the following Saturday. It was not love at first sight, but we liked each other. It seemed to be the beginning of an easy friendship.

The next day, Dick and I met at a restaurant for lunch and then went to a movie. Afterwards, I invited Dick to my house for dinner. He accepted and followed me in his car. As we drove further and further from civilization, he must have wondered where on earth I was living!

After dinner, we sat in the living room and talked and talked. I have no recollection of what we discussed for so long, but I remember suddenly looking at one of the large living room windows and saying, "Look! What is that weird, purple glow in the window? This is too far away from the city for any light-pollution."

It was the light of dawn. We had talked all night!

We didn't see each other for a few days, but the next time we were together we immediately rekindled that same easy, comfortable compatibility. With so many common interests, it seemed natural that we would begin spending more and more time together.

Inner Work

Soon we were spending weekends at my house and various weekdays at Dick's condo in town. After nearly a year, we realized that our affection had turned to love. Dick designed a rather large addition to my house and we moved in together.

It was then that Dick asked me to marry him. I told him that I felt that marriage was really just a commitment, and that since we were committed I felt we were already married. Every so often, however, he asked me again. After we had been living together for nearly five years, I said, "Listen, if we still feel this way about each other in three more years and if you still want to get married, I'll say yes, but let's not discuss it in the meantime, ok?"

He stopped asking. But three years later, to the day, he reminded me of my promise and proposed to me again. By this time, we'd been together in a committed relationship for eight years and were even more in love than before. Of course I agreed.

If I hadn't lived alone for those three years, done some inner work, and learned more about who I was and what I wanted in life, I do not believe we would have met—or, if we had, I don't think I would have recognized what a blessing our meeting was!

Dick: After we had been dating for a while, I learned that Sally had been an avid scuba diver and instructor since 1960. I suspected that if I wanted to spend vacation time with her, I had better learn to dive! So, on a long work assignment in California, I took the course and really enjoyed it (although the California water was a lot colder than the tropical seas I'd envisioned). Soon we decided that we could take a lot more scuba trips if we organized and led them. Sally, an excellent organizer, put them together. For quite a few years we led small groups around the world—to the Philippines, Australia, Papua New Guinea, Fiji, the Red Sea, and many of the best diving sites on the planet.

A few years ago I retired from my job and became a real estate broker and general contractor. Sally and I are both "frustrated architects." When we moved from Tucson to North Carolina, we really enjoyed designing and building our new, environmentally friendly house. When she's not writing articles or making jewelry, Sally continues to work as a nutritionist and health counselor, while I stay busy with building and real estate. We are both involved in civic and environmental issues.

How We Make Our Relationship Last (*Sally's version*)

Our love has grown because we maintain great mutual respect; we communicate rather than trying to control; we support each other in so many ways; we are sensitive to each other's moods and needs.

We have now been together for twenty-four years and there hasn't been a day (rarely even an hour!) that I haven't felt intensely grateful for this wonderful relationship and my wonderful husband. He is truly the greatest miracle in my life.

How We Make Our Relationship Last (*Dick's version*)

I am basically rather shy, and found that my shyness disappeared around Sally. To this day, one of the things that we most appreciate about our relationship is how our different personalities and talents fit together. Between us, we seem to be able to handle all obstacles—Sally's imagination and creativity are perfect complements to my logic and analytical capabilities.

As the years go on, our relationship grows stronger and more loving as we continue to learn and evolve together.

Inner Work

"When returning home after a long day at work, discuss positive things first. Ease into the rest of the day's challenges later."

Not a Shangri-La
Mildred and Herbert, California

*I*f not for Herb's car, he and I might never have found each other. Let me explain. In 1938, owning a car was rare. Herb had a car; I didn't, so my friend—always an opportunistic matchmaker—set us up on a blind date.

My mother and I watched Herb drive up to the house. When he walked to the door in his all-white tennis outfit, I noted the way his creamy skin stood out against his jet-black hair. He looked gorgeous.

Our first date was a picnic with friends in San Jose on July 4. We were up until midnight watching the fireworks. When Herb dropped me off, he walked me to the door.

The next morning he showed up to drive me to work, bearing flowers and candy. He was always good at remembering to shower my mother and me with gifts and thoughtful gestures. It was very smart of him to remember my mother.

Within one year, we were married. We stayed together fifty years.

One of my granddaughters asked me how you know when you've found the one. I told her, "You just do. That kind of love is very clear. You just know." I remember years later she visited me and said, "Grandma, I met the one." My granddaughter and her husband have been married six years and counting.

How We Made Our Relationship Last

My advice to anyone in love is, "Treat each other special." When returning home after a long day at work, discuss positive things first. Ease into the rest of the day's challenges later. You get dressed up for strangers; remember to get dressed up for each other, too.

Marriage is not a Shangri-La. Dating is. Dating is beautiful. Everything's new and exciting. It is completely different than marriage. You have to work at marriage like you would work at anything else in life. There is a give and take. You cannot expect everything to be perfect.

I remember one incident that occurred while my brother was visiting us. When Herb got up, I said, "Honey, could you please bring me a glass of water?"

My brother said, "Why are you being so polite? He's your husband."

I know it sounds simple but being polite is key.

We worked to figure things out together, especially with the kids. I purposely did not argue with Herb unless I thought it was very important. We had two sons and now have three granddaughters and two great-grandsons. Herb died after we celebrated our 50th anniversary in 1988.

Not a Shangri-La

"We both agreed that, had it not been for the lessons we learned from our previous relationships, we would not have been ready for each other or known exactly what we wanted."

Thank Every Prior Love

David and Burney, California

On the day that my roommate excitedly held up his published "Personals" ad, I couldn't help but notice the bold headline that was right beneath his: "Asian soul mate wanted," it read. "Do not send photo."

Gay men were trailblazers in the area of personal ads. In 1985, you could tell by the length of a personal ad if the author was looking for a serious relationship or not. Burney, the "Asian soul mate" ad's author, made it clear that he did not want to be swayed by looks. Judging from the ad's length, he also knew just what he was looking for. "You are out there," he'd written. "Here's what I already know about you."

Intrigued, I sent back a four-page reply with a sealed photo, which I instructed him to open only after reading the letter. My letter turned out to be one of four from other hopeful Asian men.

Burney is the type of guy who would rather interact in person than talk to anyone over the phone. Five minutes was a long phone conversation for Burney. He quickly decided I was too young for him, since I am eight years his junior.

Nevertheless, to his surprise, we talked for two and a half hours over the phone. We discovered that each of us had initiated the breakup of our one prior significant relationship. For me, it was a five-year relationship; for Burney, seven. We both agreed that, had it not been for the lessons we learned from our previous relationships, we would not have been ready for each other or known exactly what we wanted.

The second surprise occurred when we met in person. In his very specific ad, Burney had forgotten to mention height, assuming Asians would be short. We joke about it now—how I slipped my six-foot-two-inch frame through on a loophole.

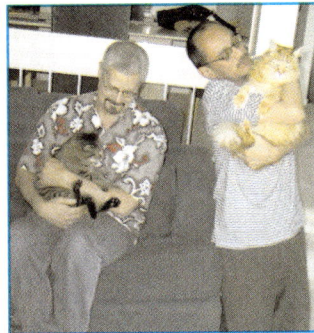

Within four months, I moved in with Burney, Katie, and Freddie (his cats). Not only was it a tiny one-bedroom apartment (a difficult adjustment for two only-children accustomed to having their own space), but I was allergic to cats. My doctor said I needed to get used to it, that my body would develop antigens. He was right. Within five or six months, my allergies went away.

How We Make Our Relationship Last

Our similarities are the reason we are still together. Being only-children creates a strong bond; our fundamental outlook on life is similar, and we have our sexual orientation in common. A lot of people want the same things, but want to go down "different roads" to get there. We, on the other hand, agree about politics, spirituality, and how we fit in the gay community.

We love to travel. We also have a certain understanding of the fact that nothing in life is perfect. I always envisioned myself sitting with a partner and flipping through the pages of a photo album that would document our journey together. Well, Burney and I are here to journey together and help one another. Each of us is like the brother the other never had.

Thank Every Prior Love

What really matters are all those underlying basics, because sex is not the most important thing in life. What we are left with over time are the other parts of the relationship that sustain us. Some of my most treasured moments, for instance, come when Burney's curled up with the cats by the fire, calling out crossword puzzle questions while I'm cooking in the kitchen.

Little things are not worth fighting about. We both have learned to "let it go." Whatever disagreements we do have are not aired in public. Early in our relationship, we fought about expectations. Burney was less demonstrative than I expected. I grew up with the notion that when you found Mr. Right, everything would be perfect, with no disagreements. In reality, you are not going to get everything you want. Nothing is taken for granted. This is the man I have chosen to be with. No one told me to be here. It was my choice. Burney says, "The secret to longevity is good planning."

Now our reward is flipping through photo albums of our journeys. On the wall, we have a framed map of the world on which we mark our travels with pushpins. Wherever our next stop is, we know one thing: We will be together as long as we are both still on this planet.

Thank Every Prior Love

"Nothing gets resolved without talking—it's childish not to talk things through."

Dancin' Fever

Mendelle and Homer, California

When we were young, big band music played on the radio on Saturday nights. One weekend, my friend Helen had to baby-sit her younger sister. During the week, she had invited some girls (and not enough boys) to come over on Saturday night. A young man whom I had been seeing was in the neighborhood on Saturday evening so she asked him if he knew any fellows he could bring over. He brought Homer and another young man.

Homer and I were attracted to each other immediately and had many interests in common: dancing, politics, lifestyle, etc. Our relationship progressed quickly. In August of the following year, we knew we were in love and became engaged. We married on February 16, 1941, with the country on the brink of World War II.

By April, Homer was in the army, frequently leaving on maneuvers, and was often gone for weeks or a month at a time. From 1942 to July 1945, he was in Europe. There was no R&R leave as there is today. Just one big ocean between us, with only letters to keep us connected for over three years. We wrote each other as often as possible, nearly every week.

When Homer returned, the transition was harder for him than for me. I was still in the same house I'd been living in when he left. He had been living solely among men, in a combat situation, which placed his very survival in jeopardy on a day-to-day basis. Homer says, "It's kinda like when you go off to camp for a few years. You have to adjust quickly." We had to get used to a whole new life together.

How We Make Our Relationship Last

Well, if I said we've been married sixty-three years without a cross word, it would make for a boring story and be a lie to boot. We've had our ups and downs like any other couple. We are attracted to each other, interested in current events, and both love music. Homer is compulsively neat and easygoing. That combination of characteristics frequently draws words from one who likes to argue (me). When we disagree, I like to talk it out loudly. Very loudly. Homer keeps his calm better than I do. He's a slow burner. We always resolve our differences. Nothing gets resolved without talking—it's childish not to talk things through. Time takes care of any hard feelings as long as you talk things over.

Having a great sense of humor is important. We can laugh at things that other couples may not be able to find funny. We always find something to talk about. Statistically, there are two primary factors that contribute to the breakup of relationships: money and children. We were not wealthy but we understood our limitations and did not complain. We lived well, but within our means. We were also very close to our in-laws. We have been fortunate, and are blessed to have each other.

"We are both over sixty and had assumed that romance was not in the cards."

One Too Many Homes

Fred and Sherrie, Okalahoma

I met my wife at a little country church in Jennings, Okalahoma (population 450). Our meeting and attraction for each other was quite a surprise, to say the least. We are both over sixty and had assumed that romance was not in the cards.

The local church had a program for disabled children to which I often took my daughter. Sherrie helped with this program (among other things) in the church. We used to sit together during services, and she would assist me with my daughter.

After about a year, Sherrie called me at my home to discuss something about the church programs. We made a date to have coffee at the mall. We talked for about three hours over a single cup.

We lived sixty-five miles away from each other, but despite the distance we would regularly meet at her home or mine just to enjoy each other's company. We discussed marriage at one point, but wanted to let our families know what was going on between us before we tied the knot.

After we told our families what we were going to do, I gave her a ring and formally asked her to marry me. I thought my heart would jump right out of my body when she said, "Yes, how about next week?" Because of our age, we decided that a long courtship was not a good idea, so we were married after just a short time together.

We then faced the challenge of consolidating two homes into one. What a mess that was! We decided to live in her home in the country and rent out my city house.

How We Make Our Relationship Last

We make compromises. I had to get used to country life. Being a city slicker, it was initially difficult, I must admit. However, I soon fell in love with the serenity of country living.

It is a fact that my heart strings are alive and vibrating at sixty-seven. Being with my soulmate has made me happier than I have ever been in my life!

One Too Many Homes

"How do individuals evolve as individuals, but also together as a couple, moving ahead even when the other is not moving at the same pace?"

California Dreamin'
Michael and Katheryn, California

*H*e played the saxophone; I played the flute (until I got kicked out of junior high band practice for laughing too much). In algebra, Michael remembers peering across the room, craning his neck to catch a glimpse of me. My abrupt and dishonorable departure from the band was a source of entertainment for him.

We dated off and on in senior high. To delve into our relationship, I need to explain the political climate of the time. In Southern Illinois during the 1960s, African Americans and whites were socially divided. There was not a lot of intermingling. Even when we would walk down the street together in small mixed groups, people would ask why I was walking with Michael. My parents received anonymous phone complaints.

My mother, president of the school board, and my father, a Presbyterian minister, were supportive of the civil rights movement. It would have been hypocritical of them to oppose my relationship. However, my decision to date Michael brought ugly realities into our home. Truth be told, my parents were holding their breath, waiting for me to graduate and move on.

Although the town of Alton was twenty percent African American, the bordering towns were all white, except for St. Louis and East St. Louis, which were predominantly black. The nearest public pool was in Wood River, a neighboring factory town, and no blacks were allowed in the pool. The surrounding atmosphere forced us to socialize in groups rather than risk being seen together as a pair.

Much to my parents' relief, I went immediately to Drake University after graduating from high school. But I only lasted a few semesters there before dropping out and returning home. My parents immediately enrolled me at the University of Missouri. After one year, I defiantly left to attend the University of Montana.

During high school, Michael's mom had gotten him a job making deliveries for the local pharmacy. After high school, Michael donned his three-piece suit, and with his five-piece band traveled from club to club in neighboring towns in the dead of winter, switching from jazz to R&B, dreaming of warm and sunny California.

We reunited in Alton seven years later thanks to our junior high school friend Rebecca, who insisted I reconnect with Michael after so many years. I was fed up with the isolation of Montana, and Michael and his band were tired of driving in unpredictable road conditions, and lugging heavy equipment from gig to gig in the middle of winter.

Soon after reuniting, we agreed to ditch the cold winters and share a VW bus ride to the West Coast—our destination highlighted on the map we used to navigate our way across country. My brother in Berkeley offered us his garage space but the band never followed.

Despite the high rent, Berkeley was exciting in 1977. The possibilities seemed endless.

Two years later, we married without the blessings of my father, who could not quite accept or sanction our marriage. It took about two years before my father finally apologized and accepted Michael.

Our daughter was born in 1984 and our son in 1988. Racism is subtler in California than in Alton, Illinois—the West Coast is a more outwardly tolerant and diverse place—but people are more curious. They stare a lot when we are together.

California Dreamin'

When we travel, we always have to consider external conditions and plan our outings and vacations accordingly. When we visit my mother's nursing home, people assume Michael is an employee or ask why he is there. Racism will always be our companion, always present.

Parenting our teenage son has occasionally created a source of conflict and an urgent and immediate need to take action and come to agreement. I have had to compromise, becoming more patient and thinking things through, acknowledging the validity of Michael's opinion during these trying times. Michael has become more flexible.

As a teenager, I was able to act out and get away with it. For my black teenage son, society's consequences could be much less forgiving. My life was filled with privileges that I took for granted. These fundamental privileges are ingrained in me. Michael looks ten years ahead and sees danger for African American males. The statistics confirm his perspective. More African American males are in prison than in college.

I believe that together we were meant to be a source of information for people, as well as a vehicle for tolerance, understanding, and acceptance.

How We Make Our Relationship Last (*Katheryn's version*)

What makes our love last is the ability to be silly and have fun together. We have gone through very difficult times and great times. My parents were together forty-seven years, so I realized at a young age that there are ups and downs in relationships. No matter what happens, I always count on—and trust—Michael's integrity. He has strong character and is a very good provider. We admire each other's core values. I depend on his grounded mentality to anchor my impulsiveness.

How We Make Our Relationship Last (*Michael's version*)

It's the core connection between us. This is inexplicable; it just is. It seems to always have been there, unspeakable, unknowable…our relationship always seemed natural.

How do individuals evolve as individuals, but also together as a couple, moving ahead even when the other is not moving at the same pace?

Words like integrity and non-traditional come to mind, as well as the ability to disrupt the status quo. Having a level of awareness and personal commitment. Also, going to our separate corners, and stepping back when we have to. Taking the time to work out our different perspectives. Becoming more mindful of each other's perspectives.

California Dreamin'

"We are both passionate people, and our passions extend to every facet of our relationship (even arguing)."

Laundry Games

Christine and Paul, Minnesota

I had just decided to give up on guys when my friend called to invite me out for a girls' night with a few of her friends. I contemplated her offer for the whole day; it was already late in the night by the time I agreed to join. We ended up going to a military bar. (My friend had access to the local base because her father was a Navy retiree.) It seemed like a good choice, since there was no chance of running into anyone we knew.

The bar was small but had a great band. We quickly grabbed a table and settled in. I had barely taken off my jacket when I was approached by a guy who struck up a conversation and asked if I wanted to dance. I shied away, but my friend agreed to dance in my place. During their dance he kept asking questions about me, and announced that he really wanted to dance with me. So when the next song came on, I thought, sure, why not? Well, as soon as we shared the slightest touch, sparks were flying. I felt—knew—that this was more than an ordinary dance.

We danced for a number of songs, until finally we both had to get something to drink. Paul retreated to his friends' table and I did likewise. Before I knew it, I was approached by one of his friends, who asked me, "What did you do to him? He said he is going to marry you." Not sure what to say, I just shrugged.

We continued to dance together, and had the best time. Around 2 a.m., the night was winding down and it was clearly time to go. Paul asked for my number. I had never given out my real phone number before, but this time I just went for it. We shared a wonderful, long kiss in the parking lot and parted ways. I had trouble getting to sleep that night. I could still smell him.

The next afternoon, I received a call from Paul. He said that he wanted to get together as soon as possible. Throughout the course of our conversation, I discovered that he was due to be shipped to his next duty station in five days. This was his last week in town!

We spent those five days together. I skipped school and work, deciding that I was going to make the most of his last few days. We had a wonderful date at the movies (he fed me popcorn). Everything just fit together—we just fit together. It wasn't about looks, it was about attraction to everything that he was (and still is).

On the third day, he phoned his mother and said that he was sitting with the girl he was going to marry. I kept thinking, Is this guy for real?

Later that week, we were at the laundromat doing his laundry and playing a game of cards. He suddenly announced that if he won the next game I would have to move with him. I lost. It was settled, though when he did leave for his next duty station (thankfully, only five hours away), I wasn't quite ready to move. We said our goodbyes, wondering what would happen next.

For a month, we phoned one another almost daily. When Paul finally returned for a visit, it was Christmas time. We spent another wonderful weekend together and then decided that this was it—we needed to be together, and we needed to get married. I went on vacation with him to meet his parents, and we went shopping for wedding rings. We had met at the beginning of November; it was only New Year's and we were already shopping for rings!

We continued our passionate long-distance relationship for a year. We were married on the military base almost exactly a year after the day we met. It was a beautiful military-style wedding with honor guards. That was

Laundry Games

nine years ago, and we are still happily married. We have three beautiful children and have moved multiple times due to my husband's military career. We are now settled in a small country town in his home state of Minnesota. I would have followed him anywhere and still would. We know that we are truly meant to be together.

How We Make Our Relationship Last

I think that our relationship works for a number of reasons. Balance is key. We are both passionate people, and our passion extends to every facet of our relationship (even arguing). We keep each other grounded. We tend to be opposite in situations—when one is down the other is up—so that we constantly compensate for each other's moods. We still have fun together as a couple and love to be with one another. We spend as much time together as we can after the kids are asleep, even if it's just time spent playing cards or watching a movie. We are each very interested in how the other's day went and we make time to talk about it. We are best friends and confide in one another. I make a point of remembering the feelings I had the night we met.

We are still very passionate about one another. My heart still beats a bit faster when I see him again after a long day at work. I still can't believe our chance encounter turned out this way, and that we are sharing our lives together.

"I was her worst nightmare. Now she's my sunny day."

My Worst Nightmare

Betty and Steve, California

etty: When I found myself in my early forties and still single, I figured I could at least enjoy reading about how others had initiated and maintained their relationships. I wanted to reach for a book of inspiring role models, but couldn't find one on bookstore shelves. I decided to compile one of my own. So I started gathering stories through casual conversations, interviews, and soliciting them via small newspaper notices.

One couple's story stood out. A woman in her forties had resolved to make a final effort before giving up on finding her life partner. She placed a personal ad in a newspaper. By the time she sent me her story, she and her husband had been married seven years. I was struck by the fact that they had lived only five minutes away from each other, but would never have met were it not for her ad.

Casting all hesitation aside, I perused the "Personals" in my local weekly paper, looking for ideas to help me compose my own ad. In the "Men Seeking Women" section, I spotted "Long-term commitment with someone willing to stick through the tough times." It was all I needed to read. I answered his ad instead of writing one.

A month later I received a voice message from a guy with a New York accent. "I was out of the country when you called," he said. "Let me know if you're still interested."

I returned his call. Following a surprisingly delightful phone conversation during which we realized that we lived only minutes apart, we decided to meet in a nearby café that weekend. As the time of our meeting drew nearer, ghosts from my failed dating experiences began to cloud my enthusiasm. I had convinced myself that the date would be a waste of a sunny day.

My first words to him were: "Can you believe we agreed to meet on such a beautiful day?" When he responded that he had been looking forward to it, I realized that I might be in for a pleasant surprise.

On our first official date about a week later, I found out that this forty-something man had never been married, had no kids, no pets—not even a houseplant. To me, these were all red flags indicating a commitment-phobic guy whom all serious women should avoid. His only redeeming quality was that he told me he loved his mother (a response to the last of my obnoxious screening questions).

When I told him that he was my worst nightmare, his response was, "Tell me more about that." Instead of running away, he challenged my preconceived notions.

As we spent more time together over the subsequent months, my cynicism dissolved into curiosity and was soon replaced by a growing sense of commitment and a mutual resolve to share our lives. We were married two years later.

With this book and a story of my own, I hope to inspire other unions and strengthen lifelong commitments.

Steve: She walked up to my table in the café and uttered her very first words to me: "Can you believe we're getting together on such a beautiful day?" She wasn't exactly complaining. But neither was she glowing about meeting indoors while it was gorgeous outside (even by Berkeley standards), with so many other things she'd rather be doing.

My Worst Nightmare

But there we were. I had placed a "Personals" ad in a local paper. She'd responded and we'd arranged to meet. Despite her reluctance, some unspoken blind date protocol seemed to discourage postponing our meeting until an uglier day. So she sat down and ordered a beer. Hmmm…that was a better sign than her initial comment. Having "done the Personals" off and on for a few years (with merely a few short-term relationships to show for it), I knew that a drink was better than a coffee at getting the conversation flowing.

And over the course of a couple of hours and a couple of beers each, it did flow. Betty (then) had a job training volunteers to provide help after natural disasters. Much like my job, consulting on democracy and access to justice abroad, summing up her work was tough. But we connected on a level that did not register at the time. As an acquaintance later pointed out to us, we were both in the "helping professions."

She also brewed beer as a hobby, had a grown son, owned a dog, and had gotten some poison oak on her arms while chasing the dog through a bramble earlier that week. And she looked good in her cute little summer dress—not that I would ever notice such a superficial thing.

After that nice talk, we shook hands and bid goodbye. I said something like, "Maybe we'll get together again." I learned later that she was expecting something more encouraging, but it all worked out.

We obviously did meet again, very soon, for dinner and a movie. We ended the evening with a sunset stroll to some Berkeley boulders overlooking the San Francisco Bay. It was again beautiful out, but this time we both were glad to be where we were.

Still, she had some understandable hesitation about me. As she put it, I was her "worst nightmare": over forty years old, never married, no kids, no pets, no plants. Not exactly signs of someone willing to commit to anything. But I loved my mother, which was good.

Our bond gradually grew over the next couple of years. I don't know when I first knew I loved her, but I do know when I first told her: about ten months after our first meeting, at sunset on a beach in Hawaii.

I also know that I am an indecisive person, but proposing marriage was the easiest decision I ever made. It wasn't even a decision, actually. At some point, I just started trying to figure out how, where, and when to propose. When the time came I carefully, nervously programmed the stereo to play a

My Worst Nightmare

romantic mix of songs, sat us down on my couch with some champagne and a sunset view, and popped the question.

Though it all seemed so natural to me, the proposal took her by surprise. Just the day before, she had told a friend that things were great with us but that she thought it would be years, if ever, before we got married.

So how did I get from avoiding commitments to proposing one? In lots of ways:

Learning from previous relationships, though I didn't know it at the time. This included the lesson that, as a Bruce Springsteen song puts it, "You can't shut off the risk and the pain without losing the love that remains."

Also, having a good friend tell me what I didn't want to hear: that when it came to romance, I was becoming even more of a perfectionist with age, and that it was keeping me from my goal of settling down.

And timing: As much as I know we're right for each other, the timing also had to be right. Both Betty and I had to be ready to share the compromises and challenges that life would throw at us, and to embrace the fact that love involves effort rather than simply living happily ever after. Or to put it another way, to realize that living happily ever after involves effort.

Most of all, of course, there's Betty: her energy, her joy, her smile. I was her worst nightmare. Now she's my sunny day.

How We Make Our Relationship Last (*Betty's version*)

Tips from other committed couples help me stay creative and have taught me to appreciate my relationship. I used to avoid talking about difficult topics, wishing they would magically go away. One of the strengths of our relationship is our willingness to address difficult issues before they fester. On the other hand, I've also learned that it is often best not to grapple with such matters when we are both tired.

Tension dissipates when one of us backs down in the middle of a heated discussion by acknowledging that the other person may actually be right or by asking what is really motivating the argument. It helps to talk when the heat of the moment has subsided. All it sometimes takes is one of us to change the tempo (for instance, to make a joke when we are taking ourselves too seriously) and issues seem to melt away.

Steve continually surprises me with thoughtful notes, making special dinners, and dancing with me in the living room. He always makes our alone time a priority and remembers to tell me when he thinks loving thoughts. I love how he gets up from whatever he is doing and greets me when I walk in the front door. These small but important actions help nour-ish and enliven our love in ways I never thought possible. They are infec-tious, too. The more I receive, the more I give back. Steve has taught me how to keep the magic in our love.

How We Make Our Relationship Last (*Steve's version*)

So what makes our love last? Talking about our hopes and dreams, fears and frustrations, and what is going on with the two of us. For me, that includes getting over the typical "guy thing" of bottling up my thoughts inside my head. I've finally learned that I feel better when I let them out and get her feedback. For Betty, it means getting past the (less severe but still noteworthy) "gal thing" of wanting all communication all the time, and see-ing that there are times to strike a balance.

We rarely fight. But when we do, we make up once the flash of anger has passed, rather than letting it simmer. Ever hear those famous words from that old movie, *Love Story*: "Love means never having to say you're sorry"? Wrong. Love means sometimes saying you're sorry because doing so is often more important than determining who was right or wrong.

Embracing and enjoying our differences. I'm often slow to figure out what I want to do and then to do it. She sometimes moves from thought to action in the time it takes to read a sentence. Thanks to Betty, we got our act together to look for and buy a house we both love. Thanks to me, that house is close to our work, friends, and family in California, rather than in rural New Zealand.

There's more. Friendship. Fun. Laughter. Spontaneity. Surprises. Shared values. Shared sunsets. Regularly telling each other, "I love you."

We each also have our own idiosyncratic ways of keeping our love fresh. I came of age with Bruce Springsteen's music. Even as that music has evolved from youthful angst to spirited middle-aged wisdom, it has kept inspiring me. As for Betty, long before we met she was interviewing all the commit-ted couples she knew in order to find out what made their relationships work. She continues to draw on what she learned along her road to love. As do I. And so, I hope, will you.

My Worst Nightmare

Toolbox of Tips
by Betty Lucas

A Toolbox for Couples

Online dating and other organized ways of finding lifelong partners are fast becoming national pastimes, even as the United States divorce rate hovers at fifty percent. More and more people are seeking lasting love while half of the country's couples are unable to keep their love alive. I believe that most committed couples can thrive once they learn which specific tools can help them overcome obstacles.

Many Roads to Love is partly a collection of relationship role models. There is no substitute for the examples and inspiration that its stories provide. But after interviewing more than 200 couples and individuals over the years, I've distilled some core lessons into this "Toolbox for Couples."

Every couple is unique. Choose which tools work for you in order to build or rebuild the relationship of your dreams.

1) **Create Positive Moments**: Focus on what works in your relationship and why. Compliments and expressions of affection take so little effort and cause so much happiness. Plus, kind words and gestures are infectious. The more positive loving moments you have to fall back on during the lean times, the more resilient is your love.

2) **Express Your Needs**: Tell each other what you need in order to feel loved or appreciated. What works for each of you? Do you need to hear words, be touched, receive tangible things? Discover the "Instruction Manual" of what makes your partner happy.

3) **Air Issues Constructively**: A problem does not go away if it is bottled up; it just festers. The most successful method of resolving an issue is to begin by airing it in a constructive, solution-oriented fashion. Respectful starts in dealing with difficulties increase your odds for happy endings or resolving issues.

4) **Make Peace Offerings**: A key to relationship longevity is to shorten the duration of arguments and strive to heal after they occur, rather than

allowing the hurt to linger. Healing can begin by offering your partner some understanding, a gesture, an apology, a hug. Learn what offerings work.

5) **State Facts:** Talk about problems in terms of specific facts you experience (i.e., "I felt hurt when you said/did that") rather than finger-pointing, assigning blame, or name-calling.

6) **Watch Transition Times:** If certain circumstances or times of the day spur discord (for instance, when you are sleep-deprived, just home from work, or in some other transition mode), agree to STOP and discuss tough topics during less vulnerable times.

7) **Dig Deep:** When the same disagreement keeps surfacing with no apparent solution or compromise, dig deeper to identify core feelings. Be open to hidden truths and new perspectives.

8) **Let It Go:** The importance of compromise almost goes without saying. But it also can be important to find what you cannot change in the circumstance or your partner. Accept it, and leave behind the urge to revive issues or remake her/him.

9) **Keep Support Networks:** Divorce rates decrease when couples have strong support networks. Couples lacking such networks may want to increase their involvement in community or group activities.

10) **Anticipate Problems:** Discuss and agree on your boundaries and/or limits ahead of time, rather than at the moment the issue arises. Such discussions can prevent arguments about money, parenting, religion, in-laws, vacations, etc.

Relationship Stages and Cycles: Every long-term relationship goes beyond the blissful, you-can-do-no-wrong (honeymoon) stage. Love and feelings naturally evolve. It can help to understand the stages that many couples experience over time and the cycles that repeat during major life transitions:

1) **Bliss:** Everything is new. Similarities and differences seem complementary.

2) **Not-so-bliss:** Differences begin to irritate and disappoint.

3) **If Only**: If only you were more like me. If only I could change you back to whom I thought you were. A power struggle may ensue.

4) **Understanding**: Understand that the end of the blissful honeymoon stage can give way to a deeper, equally wonderful love, but that it may involve mutual effort. Also understand the need for balance between time spent together and apart.

5) **Acceptance**: Accept or even embrace differences. Learn to live happily together in recognition of the fact that neither partner is perfect.

A Toolbox for Singles

This "Toolbox" is a compilation of tips for people interested in building rewarding, lasting relationships. It is for the single person open to a relationship, actively seeking one, or getting involved with someone new.

1) **Notice What Works in Your Life**: Focus on aspects of your single life that are working rather than on what is not. Positive experiences breed more of the same. Make the best of what is in the moment, keeping your interests alive. People are drawn to those who have interests and live their passions.

2) **Look Inside**: Do not look to others to make you happy or wait for someone to fill what's missing in your life. You are the main course; relationships are life's dessert.

3) **Give Love**: Give the love you wish to receive. Treat yourself as you hope to be treated. If you have never felt love or if you lack lasting love, make one change in your life, spend time around someone less fortunate, take up a hobby, or befriend a pet. Animals not only teach love and provide company, studies have shown the act of petting an animal is healthful.

4) **Find Role Models**: Whether you actively seek a partner or not, remain open to the possibility of a lasting relationship and observe healthy relationship role models. These are good first steps while you pursue your life's interests and passions.

5) **List Your Wishes**: Lists can serve as useful guidelines (though not rules). The simple act of writing down your desires or stating your intentions can set wheels in motion and clarify what you think you want. Write down qualities you might be looking for in a mate: romantic, social, affectionate, introspective, etc. Conversely, list lessons you've learned, qualities you wish to avoid, or signs you ignored in previous relationships. Your lists may help you establish new patterns or keep you from repeating old ones.

6) **Watch for Red Flags**: Early in relationships, warnings or red flags may emerge but be ignored. Discuss your priorities and ask questions when you notice compatibility issues. Listen carefully. Pay attention to actions, as opposed to what you hope to see and hear.

7) **Maintain Community**: Maintain friendships and your personal community as new relationships evolve. Strong community ties are important for healthy, long-term relationships. Make conscious choices about what you stop doing to make room for someone new in your life, rather than letting yourself drift away from other people who are important to you.

8) **Slow Down**: Take your time with intimacy. Rushing intimacy can be a cover for insecurity. Ask yourself, why the rush? Break through patterns that haven't worked in the past. Do something different.

9) **Seek Balance**: Are your activities equally divided among your and his/her interests or are they one-sided? Does this balance work for you?

10) **Express your needs**. Tell each other what you need in order to feel loved or appreciated. What works for each of you? Do you need to hear words, be touched, receive tangible things? Discover the "Instruction Manual" of what makes you and your new partner happy.

I hope this book and these "Toolboxes" help you find and stay on your own Road to Love and Happiness.

About the Author

Betty Lucas coaches couples and individuals to help them obtain desired, lasting change in their lives. Over the past decade, she has interviewed more than 200 couples about their relationships and collected stories and advice from many of them. *Many Roads to Love* is a labor of love and a tool Betty uses in her coaching. She can testify to the inspirational and practical value of love stories; after all, it was another couple's story that put her on the road to finding the love of her life. *Many Roads to Love* is the first book in Betty's Many Roads series.

To purchase this book, visit www.manyroads.net.

To contact the author with any comments about *Many Roads to Love* or to submit your story for consideration for the second edition of *Many Roads to Love*, e-mail betty@manyroads.net.

SPECIAL OFFER – "Book-Plus-One-Story"

Any couple interested in having their story included as the first chapter in *Many Roads to Love*, creating their own personalized edition, can purchase Betty's "Book-Plus-One-Story" option. For story and photo guidelines, visit www.manyroads.net.

(A minimum purchase of ten books is required for this option.)

GIVE THE GIFT OF LOVE TO LAST A LIFETIME
Many Roads to Love

Valentine's Day

Anniversaries

Birthdays

Weddings